AUSTRALIAN
WILDFLOWER FAIRIES

This edition published 2018
By Living Book Press

1st edition published by Consolidated Press Ltd. Sydney 1937
Revised edition published 1945

ISBN: 978-0-6481048-4-1

A catalogue record for this
book is available from the
National Library of Australia

AUSTRALIAN WILDFLOWER FAIRIES

by

NURI MASS

BOTANICAL	FAIRY
ILLUSTRATIONS	ILLUSTRATIONS
by	by
NURI MASS	CELESTE MASS

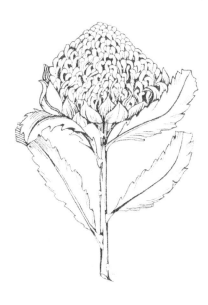

ALSO BY NURI MASS

Virginia Woolf, The Novelist (M.A. Thesis, Sydney Univ. 1942)
    Magazine Features, published under Tina Banks nom-de-plume;
- Magic Circle
- Babe in the Woods
- Such Little Things
- The Visit
- Neighbour-Wise
- The Uninvited
- Article - Virginia Woolf
- Review - Tomorrow is Theirs
- It Couldn't Fail
- Spotlight Getaway
- Russian Mystery
- His Happiness
- The Parcel
- Foxy and I
- Fallen Leaf
- The Reason Why
- There Was, Once Upon a Time...

The Little Grammar People
The Wizard of Jenolan
Magic Australia
The Silver Candlestick
Where the Incas Trod
Randy Blair
The Wonderland of Nature
Many Paths - One Heaven
China the Waking Giant
Australian Wildflower Magic
Flowers of the Australian Alps
The Gift
Donna Roon
As Much Right To Live
Don't Kill It - It's Me
Just Give Us Time

BY CELESTE MASS

Little Miss Snipit

BY NURI MASS AND CELESTE MASS

The Australian Children's World (magazine)

*Very lovingly do I dedicate this book to my darling
MOTHER,
and also to all young Nature-lovers.*

PREFACE

Although increased interest in our native flora has recently been developed in our primary schools, much remains to be done in training the young minds to appreciate the structure and habits of our common trees, shrubs and herbs. This appreciation will never be acquired, particularly by primary school children, by mere factual instruction. It must come through an appeal to the child's emotional, imaginative and spiritual qualities—such is the purpose of this book.

The publication is unique in our Botanical and Nature Study literature, inasmuch as the numerous common trees, shrubs and herbs are invested with fairy-like qualities which will appeal to teacher and pupil alike. And how admirably adapted for such fairy lore are our little delicate Orchids, our glorious Christmas Bush, our ubiquitous Eucalypts and Wattles, our stately Waratah, and the other unique proteaceous plants! Each story has a "moral," and knowledge and appreciation of the outstanding characters of the plants will unconsciously and surely eventuate as the stories are read and appreciated. The stories are interesting and romantic, the language simple, fanciful and effective. Most of the stories are supplemented by delightfully expressed stanzas emphasising the outstanding characteristics of the plant, and for the benefit of the teacher and the pupils in the higher classes, excellent drawings and simple botanical descriptions are included. The functions of botanical structures are continually emphasised.

This publication is more than an acquisition to our Nature Study literature; it is a milestone along the path of desirable educational methods in our infant and primary schools.

E. BREAKWELL,

8/11/37

Inspector of Schools.

INTRODUCTION

My dear little Reader,—

Of course, you know that every bushland flower has a fairy all to itself. In reality, cityland flowers have fairies also, but in the city there are so many people hurrying about all day long, most of them having nothing whatsoever to do with fairies, calling them "nonsense" and other terrible names like that, that they have been frightened away; and although they do sometimes enter a mortal garden to love and protect those whose names and appearance they bear, they live nearly always high above the earth and above the clouds in a beautiful place called Fairyland.

But in the bush—in those dark, mossy, secret nooks where mortals very seldom venture, and also hidden in the grasses of the open country—throngs of tiny, shimmering fairies love to dwell, with those delicate flowers who are just as shy and timid as they; for fairies, as you know, are the souls of flowers!

Now, quite a short time ago, at that dark blue hour of twilight, I happened to be walking through a very quiet, unvisited portion of our bush, and I was thinking of many things—but principally of fairies. And the more I thought the sadder I grew, for I remembered what shy wee creatures they were, and how careful they had to be never to be seen by mortal eyes.

"Alas," said I aloud to myself, "how very unfortunate are humans—and how unhappy am **I**, being a human!"

But as sorrow always serves to make us weary, I began to feel all of a sudden as if I could walk no farther; so I sat down on a little bank of green grass, and, for no particular reason at all, picked two or three Bluebells that were growing nearby.

Now, the night was becoming darker and more magic every minute—and, of course, I must have shaken those Bluebells a good deal as I picked them. So I dare say you can imagine for yourself what happened. All the wildflower fairies, hovering about not **very** far away, had heard the tiny tinkling of bells; and almost as soon as I had picked the fairy flowers, I saw a rapid movement through the grass. Then my eye alighted on a little yellow Orchid—then I saw a green and a pink one. Beside them was a shrub covered with Mountain Devil flowers, and creeping over it a long strand of snowy Clematis. In fact, there were so many flowers all around me, that I thought the whole bush was trying to crowd on to my bank of green grass.

They looked stationary enough, but in reality they were all disturbed! I knew it, and I told them so. Upon hearing that I loved them and did not want to hurt them, but to be made their immediate friend, they gradually began to peep out with shiny little fairy eyes—yes! they **were** fairies! And one by one, they told me their sweet stories, and sang me the prettiest songs.

And it was because I felt sure that you also would love to hear them that I have written them down for you, just the way I heard them myself.

I do hope you are going to enjoy them as I did.

—NURI MASS.

A NOTE FROM THE AUTHOR'S CHILDREN

We have updated this edition, coming about 80 years after our 18-year old mother wrote the original version, to give more detail in some areas. We have:

- appended her flower diagram from "The Wonderland of Nature" to show the names of flower parts, shown in the Contents under "Diagram of a Flower";
- changed the sex of the 'worker bees' that visit flowers to female, since male 'drone' bees generally stay in their hives until their mating flight;
- updated some flower names; and
- described in more detail how plants make sugars, and what a 'kino' is.

At the time this book was first published and became a recommended school textbook, its imaginative images and storylines fitted in well with those of contemporaneous Australian author-artists such as May Gibbs and Ida Rentoul Outhwaite. We do hope that now, retaining this old-world reverence for the magic in our unique Australian bushland, this book can find a new enchanted audience and help us to better understand and cherish our natural world.

Tess and Chris Horwitz

2018

CONTENTS

FAIRY

ILLUSTRATIONS

"What very pleasant weather!"

The Knight of the Fairy Garter

(CRYPTOSTYLIS—type subulata)

Red and yellow and green and brown,
My name, Cryptostylis subulata;
Bold and daring I stand erect:
I am the Knight of the Fairy Garter!

Yes, indeed, I am a very noble Orchid, and I am always accomplishing such chivalrous deeds that all my Orchid relations seem to look up to me a great deal.

Do you see the large dark green leaf (as people call it) which I wear at the bottom of my plant? Well, in reality, that is my shield, and it is a great protection for me, as you can well imagine. Unlike most of my relations, I only have one very significant petal. It is called my "labellum"; and as I am so proud of my honourable title, I wear my garter in the form of three little black stripes from one end of it nearly to the other.

And talking about relations, I can tell you a secret about them. I think they are rather sensitive of it, for none of them ever mention a word of it— but nearly all of them stand up-side-down, that is to say, on their heads. Personally, I think it a little undignified, and that is another reason why I am so different and why I gain such respect; I stand on my feet! For my part, I have never heard of a noble achieving such distinction as Knight of the Garter on his head, have you?

I suppose it is partly because I realise the great majesty of my position that I do not bother to arrive in perfect time, and mostly make my appearance a little late. A quarter-past Summer is far more becoming, I think, than five minutes to spring.

I am an enthusiastic listener of every passing breeze's symphony and the glory of the bush-birds' choir; also a keen spectator of every butterfly's toe-dancing exhibition. If you wish to meet me in Nature's theatre, you will usually find me with several of my own family in the dress-circle, sitting in grassy seats on the very tops of hills.

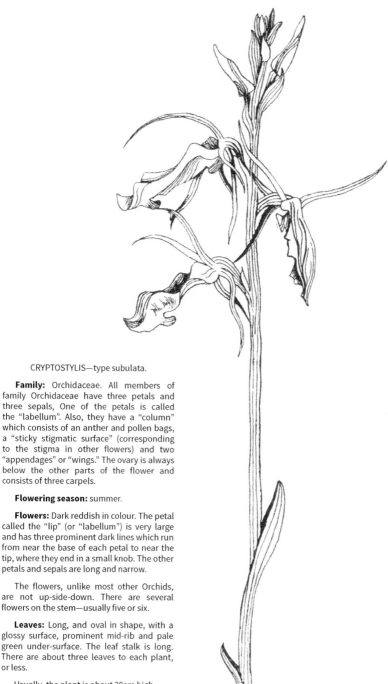

CRYPTOSTYLIS—type subulata.

Family: Orchidaceae. All members of family Orchidaceae have three petals and three sepals, One of the petals is called the "labellum". Also, they have a "column" which consists of an anther and pollen bags, a "sticky stigmatic surface" (corresponding to the stigma in other flowers) and two "appendages" or "wings." The ovary is always below the other parts of the flower and consists of three carpels.

Flowering season: summer.

Flowers: Dark reddish in colour. The petal called the "lip" (or "labellum") is very large and has three prominent dark lines which run from near the base of each petal to near the tip, where they end in a small knob. The other petals and sepals are long and narrow.

The flowers, unlike most other Orchids, are not up-side-down. There are several flowers on the stem—usually five or six.

Leaves: Long, and oval in shape, with a glossy surface, prominent mid-rib and pale green under-surface. The leaf stalk is long. There are about three leaves to each plant, or less.

Usually, the plant is about 38cm high.

The Mountain Devil

(LAMBERTIA—type formosa)

Do you know what it is like to be trapped in a huge jungle, where everything is tangled together and trying to tangle round you too?

Well, if you could be like Alice in Wonderland, and have some of the things happening to you that once happened to her, you would perhaps eat a little piece of mushroom which would make you grow smaller and smaller, until you were only the size of an ant.

Maybe you would think that exciting. But there are always faults to be found, even in the choicest of adventures. And so, being the size of a little brown ant, you would most likely feel inclined to get into all the mischief that an ant gets into. And one of the very first things you would do would be to sniff round a little and say to yourself:

"Honey! I smell honey! And I am very fond of honey!" Then, you would set out to find it, only to discover that it was lying hidden away, deep down in my flower.

You would be rather careless after this and, not taking as a hint the fact that I had concealed it so carefully, you would begin your dangerous descent down my little tunnel of flame-coloured petals. And what would you meet there? Why! You would find yourself in a dark, dense jungle of—oh, all sorts of creepy, frightening things. They would only be a number of soft, fluffy hairs in reality. But you, being so small, would think otherwise, and would realise for the first time that you were not wanted.

Of course, you would try ever so hard to escape then. You would stumble over one hair, and fall on your head over another, and turn a double somersault over the next.

But in the end, you would manage to get out, and, feeling yourself once more in the open air, you would look back at me and threaten me a good deal, and say that without any doubt I was a huge, or an immense, or a "mountainous" devil!

I wonder if that is truly why I am called the "Mountain Devil," or whether my name also comes from the fact that my home is often on the hills and mountain-tops?

Of course, although I admit that I am somewhat of a devil in my own way, I must make you feel certain, little reader, that I am not of the really

HONEY FLOWER or MOUNTAIN DEVIL.

(LAMBERTIA—type formosa)

Family: Proteaceae. Australia is famous for this group of plants which are not found anywhere else except in South Africa.

Flowering season: Throughout the year.

Flowers: Red in colour and tubelike. In the opened flower four free parts are seen: these parts and the inside of the tube being covered with hairs, which prevent unwanted insects from entering. Four stamens are placed on the petals. In the flower the pistil stands out far beyond the petal parts. There are usually six or seven blooms in a group at the end of the stem, surrounded by little satiny leaves, called "bracts", which entirely cover the buds. Honeysuckers usually carry the pollen from flower to flower, and they can therefore be called "pollinators".

Fruit: A woody box, whose peculiar shape gave the name of "Mountain Devil." This box contains two seeds which have wings.

villainous type; for a flower or a fairy could never be cruel. I am fond of mischief, that's all. My whole existence is mischief, you know—even to the beautiful colours of my flowers, and the satiny leaves that protect them when they are still buds. Because, just when human visitors to bushland are thinking how sweet and harmless I appear, I begin to drop my satiny leaves (which botanists call "bracts") and also my flame-coloured petals, leaving only a funny, fantastic-looking little head, which is green at first, but which gets hard and brown as it grows larger.

It has a long, pointed nose, and two long, pointed horns. (You can see its portrait on the previous page).

Naturally, when they pass me again a few days afterwards and see what has happened, they are absolutely bewildered, and they whisper stories about my being a devil in disguise.

Then, when they come up to look at me more closely, I cannot resist the temptation to prick their fingers or noses with the sharp, needle-like ends of my foliage leaves.

Oh, you should see how they jump when this happens—and get away as quickly as possible, without even looking back to see how my whole bush is simply shaking with laughter.

Some flowers, I know, like to make their appearance only in one or two seasons of the year. For me, that would seem a most unexciting form of existence—especially as my flowers are my chief helpers in mischief-making.

And that is why you will probably see several bright splashes of red and orange colour on my bushes whenever you happen to pass me—regardless of time or weather.

Be careful, be careful, little human child!
The woods are weird and haunted,
The woods are strange and wild.
A tiny Mountain Devil may spring upon your path,
And with his fiery eye
May ask the reason why
You've chanced within his secret haunts.
And if your answer is not good,
Or if he has not understood,
He'll quickly grab you by the hair
And drag you to a goblin's lair!
And after this you'll never go
Too near where Mountain Devils grow!

"Became a little azure flower."

The Twilight Fairy

(THELYMITRA——type grandiflora)

Although humans mostly call me the Great Sun Orchid, amongst the fairy-folk I am always known as the Orchid of Twilight; for indeed, my blooms, which are large and numerous, are very much like the sky at twilight—that deep velvety blue, almost purple colour, still tinged with the golden kiss of a lingering sunbeam.

And do you know how this came about in the very beginning? Well, then, I shall tell you:

> One evening when the sky was blue,
> And tinted with a rosy hue,
> A host of tiny fairy things
> On starry dust-besprinkled wings
> Flew up above the clouds of snow,
> Beyond our mortal sight, and lo!
> There fell upon the earth well nigh
> Ten million pieces of the sky—
> Which each, through mystic fairy power,
> Became a little azure flower.
> Alas! The elves complaining came;
> "The sky will never be the same,
> With all the holes that you have left
> Through sheer destruction-love and theft!"
> The fairies laughed in happy glee:
> "Oh, silly ones, you soon will see;
> For fairies could not beauty mar"—
> Each space became a twinkling star!

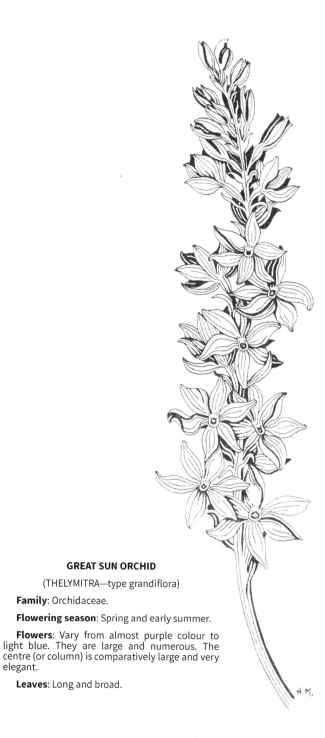

GREAT SUN ORCHID

(THELYMITRA—type grandiflora)

Family: Orchidaceae.

Flowering season: Spring and early summer.

Flowers: Vary from almost purple colour to light blue. They are large and numerous. The centre (or column) is comparatively large and very elegant.

Leaves: Long and broad.

The Lament of the Sundew Fairy

(DROSERA—type binata)

In the kingdom of flowers and fairies, I am sorry to say that I belong to Cannibal Island. Perhaps little human boys may think that a most exciting home, filled to the brim with adventures. But, strange as it may seem, I am a sad and lonely wildflower—because, you see, I am the cannibal.

Now, if you listen to my story I think you will understand how it is that I do such cruel things, and that I am left so very much alone by all the fairy-folk.

Doubtless you have often heard your human friends mention the name Sundew. Well, that means me—or else one of my near relations. The name is really a good one, I think, because when the sun shines down on me, my long, forked leaves look just as if they were covered with crystal dewdrops. As you can imagine, they are very pretty indeed. All humans think they are, and so do flies, ants and other tiny insects.

But here is where the tragic part begins. Those little sparkling things are not dewdrops at all. They are the sticky ends of simply dozens of long, fine hairs.

Now, when Sir Fly or William Ant, Esq. comes along to admire them, they immediately chuckle to themselves and with a loud shout (which mortals never heat, but which I always do hear) of "Ha! Trapped!" they close down all over their poor wee victim, holding him tightly, as if with a hundred strong arms. Of course, he cannot possibly breathe, and so in a very few minutes he dies, and my plant eats him up.

Oh, the heart of my flower sinks with sorrow when this happens, but it can never do anything to save the lives of inquisitive insects who will go inspecting my attractive leaves.

Often and often I hold up my five petals (which have grown so pale with worry that they are now milky white) and warn passing small beetles, flies, mosquitoes, and so on:

"Oh, please, do not go near my leaves, little friends. You will go to your death! You will go to your death!"

But they look back at me over their shoulders, and call out their answer to me:

"Silly, timid flower! We're not afraid of anything—just watch us. We're not afraid!"

And with this, of course, they daringly alight upon those cruel, deceiving "dewdrops." And in the next morning's "Bushland News" there appears a startling account of the heart-rending deaths of Mademoiselle Mosquito and Senor Beetle at the hands of cannibal Sundew.

No wonder elves and fairies shun my company. No wonder I am the loneliest and saddest of all wildflowers!

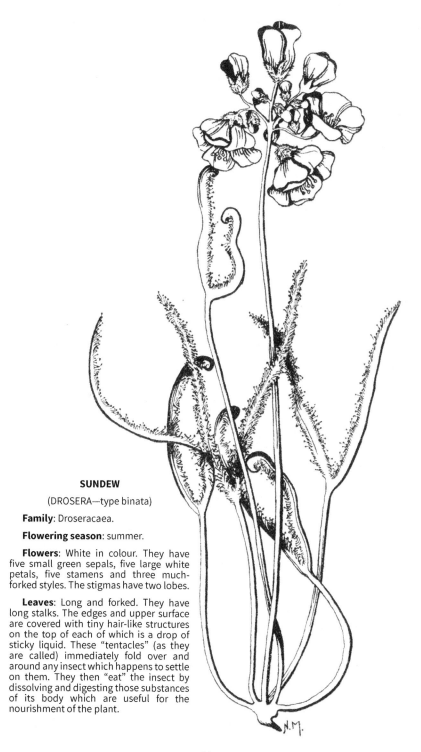

SUNDEW

(DROSERA—type binata)

Family: Droseracaea.

Flowering season: summer.

Flowers: White in colour. They have five small green sepals, five large white petals, five stamens and three much-forked styles. The stigmas have two lobes.

Leaves: Long and forked. They have long stalks. The edges and upper surface are covered with tiny hair-like structures on the top of each of which is a drop of sticky liquid. These "tentacles" (as they are called) immediately fold over and around any insect which happens to settle on them. They then "eat" the insect by dissolving and digesting those substances of its body which are useful for the nourishment of the plant.

21

The Boronia Fairy
(BORONIA—type ledifolia)

Sometimes I cannot help wishing that I was only a common little weed, prized by fairies and despised by humans; for, in that case, my life would be much happier than it is.

Somebody called "the Government" (about whom I know very little indeed) has declared me "protected," and has forbidden people from picking me without special permission. But I am afraid my life is almost as perilous as it would be if I were not protected at all, because people just do not seem to take much notice of what the Government says.

Quite often, of course, poor humans come along and gather great armfuls of me to sell in the city streets to rich humans. I do not resent this in the slightest (as long as they pick me when I am growing in gardens) for although sometimes the smoke and dust of busy streets nearly choke me, I know that I am helping to buy food and clothing for those who are really in need. And my heart simply bounds for joy when I am carried into a room where someone is lying ill, because, although again I find it difficult not to choke with all the queer unpleasant odours filling the air, I know that I am bringing happiness to one who may be sad.

But when cruel, thoughtless mortals come tramping down the bush-tracks, doing nothing except destroying everywhere they go, my whole plant quivers with fear, and my bright pink flowers try in vain to hide amongst the bushes surrounding them. Mostly I have great cause for fear, because the next moment I find myself being whisked along the track—high up in the air or dragged along the ground—far, far away from my happy home. And I have not been picked with any regard to my feelings either, but pulled up by my very roots—which is a most terrible and lamentable thing. You would think so too if it happened to you.

So you can see what a dangerous and uncertain existence a prized bush-flower has to live, and why I began by telling you that at times I wished I was only a common little weed, can't you?

Now although we Boronias are Australian plants some of the other members of our family are very fond of life on the Continent. These are what people call the citrus fruits—like oranges, lemons and mandarins. You may be surprised to hear that I have a lemon for my cousin, because we look so very different from one another. But if you examine us again closely,

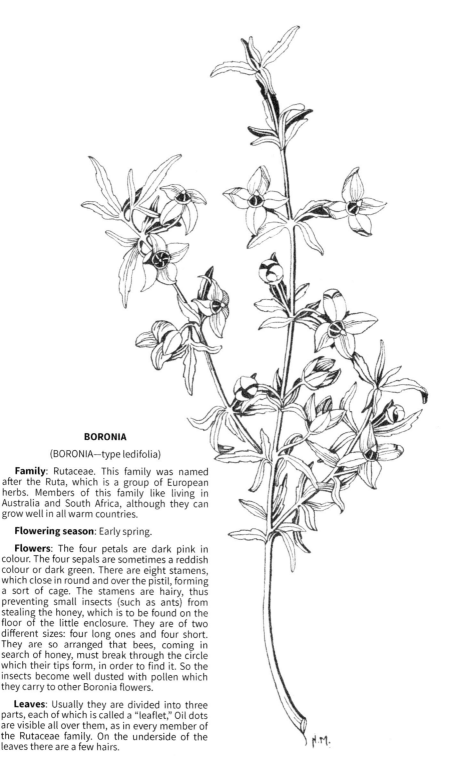

BORONIA

(BORONIA—type ledifolia)

Family: Rutaceae. This family was named after the Ruta, which is a group of European herbs. Members of this family like living in Australia and South Africa, although they can grow well in all warm countries.

Flowering season: Early spring.

Flowers: The four petals are dark pink in colour. The four sepals are sometimes a reddish colour or dark green. There are eight stamens, which close in round and over the pistil, forming a sort of cage. The stamens are hairy, thus preventing small insects (such as ants) from stealing the honey, which is to be found on the floor of the little enclosure. They are of two different sizes: four long ones and four short. They are so arranged that bees, coming in search of honey, must break through the circle which their tips form, in order to find it. So the insects become well dusted with pollen which they carry to other Boronia flowers.

Leaves: Usually they are divided into three parts, each of which is called a "leaflet," Oil dots are visible all over them, as in every member of the Rutaceae family. On the underside of the leaves there are a few hairs.

23

you will see that we really are alike in many things. The formation of our flowers is similar, in spite of the fact that orange- and lemon-blossoms have five petals and sepals whilst I have only four, and also different numbers of stamens from mine.

And there is something else by which you can always recognise a member of my family (Rutaceae by name) when you see it. If you hold the leaves of a Rutaceae plant up to the light, you will notice all over them tiny round specks of a whitish colour. These are, in reality, little glands filled with oil. This oil gives the plant a strange scent which, because it is disliked by animals that live on herbs, helps to protect the plant against them and the damage they might cause.

Have you ever noticed the funny little cage that my stamens form around my pistil? If not, you should look for it next time you come across me, as it is worth seeing. Each wee stamen is a separate bar. In this way, the pistil is well protected from the heat and brightness of day.

Now, on the floor of the cage is the honey; and when Ms. Bee comes along to take her share of it, she must push her head down through the circle formed by my anthers, in order to find it. So that when, after quite a little while, she drags her head out again, she looks as funny as anything—just as if she were wearing a yellow powdered wig. We flowers laugh at her ever so much; but, owing to the honey she has quaffed, she is feeling in merry mood, and gaily buzzes off to another pink bloom without the slightest offence.

"Ungrateful he, who pluck'd thee from thy stalk,
Poor faded flow'ret! On his careless way;
Inhal'd awhile thy odours on his walk,
Then onward pass'd and left thee to decay.

Ah! melancholy emblem! had I seen
Thy modest beauties dew'd with Evening's gem,
I had not rudely cropp'd thy parent stem,
But left thee, blushing, 'mid the enliven'd green."

—Coleridge.

The Song of the Blackberry Fairy

(RUBUS—type fruticosus)

A restless and mischievous wildflower am I,
As white as the clouds in the clear azure sky.
My home is now here, my home is now there—
My home, to speak truly, is 'most everywhere.
An elegant bramble I never could be:
Politest society shudders at me,
For ne'er was there anyone under the sun
Enamoured, as I am, of mischief and fun!

A delicate morsel, for instance, are socks,
And pieces of petticoats, jackets and frocks.
As children are passing, upon them I seize—
And mostly they leave me a bit of their knees.
But frightful discomfiture everyone knows
If e'er I should catch at the tip of his nose.
For pleasure untold is a little hooked thorn,
Yet mortals think only of things that it's torn.

But I am forgiven—and even by **them**
When black, luscious berries appear on each stem!

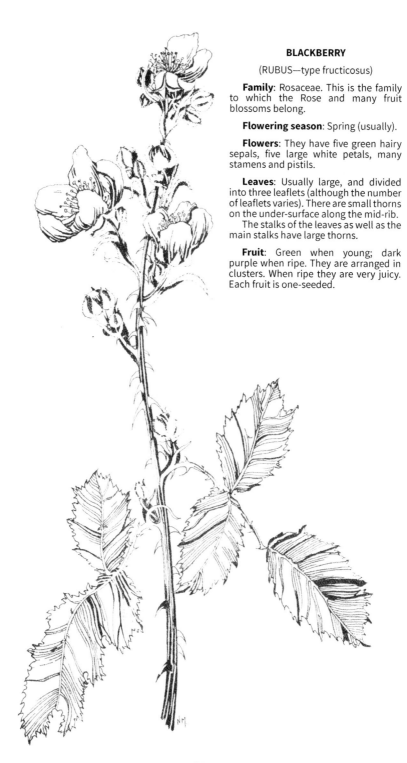

BLACKBERRY

(RUBUS—type fructicosus)

Family: Rosaceae. This is the family to which the Rose and many fruit blossoms belong.

Flowering season: Spring (usually).

Flowers: They have five green hairy sepals, five large white petals, many stamens and pistils.

Leaves: Usually large, and divided into three leaflets (although the number of leaflets varies). There are small thorns on the under-surface along the mid-rib.
The stalks of the leaves as well as the main stalks have large thorns.

Fruit: Green when young; dark purple when ripe. They are arranged in clusters. When ripe they are very juicy. Each fruit is one-seeded.

The Wild Parsley Fairy

(LOMATIA—type silaifolia)

You take it quite for granted that birds, bees, moths and butterflies have wings, do you not? And yet, I wonder if you have ever thought of flowers as having them, too? Indeed, so usual is it to consider the plant world as stationary, that even flowers themselves forget sometimes, and bemoan their adventure-less existences.

But now, when you start to think about it a little, you will realise that there are some plants which are to be found not only in one country but throughout many others as well. How, then, can anyone imagine that their whole lives are spent in the one spot and in the one little piece of soil?

"Oh," I can hear you answering me, "That is easy to explain. The plant grows and dies exactly where it has been sown. Then, next year, seeds grow into other plants, which in their turn live exactly where they have been sown."

But you must be careful not to think of these little seeds as being something quite apart from the plant which you are able to see, holding its leaves and branches up in the golden sunlight, and thrusting its roots into the dark soil. For, since they are formed actually inside the flowers of those plants, they must be just as much a part of them as are the flowers themselves.

And now, if we should follow the journeyings of ripe wee seeds which have broken away from their long imprisonment, we would surely never think again that a plant's whole life is one of inactivity.

Some seeds, when they gain their freedom, like to fly—others to float, others to swim, and others are so lazy that they depend on being carried away by passing animals, to whose furry coats they cling as tightly as they can with tiny needle-like structures and spikes.

But since, of all these and many other ways, my seeds always prefer to fly, I am naturally more interested in that form of travelling than in any of the rest.

Flying, of course, needs wings or (in my case as well as in numerous others) only one wing, so that, attached to the end of each of my seeds, you will see a long, brown, papery structure which answers my purpose well, and by means of which my seed is able to travel extensively and see quite a lot of the bush before it settles down and decides to grow.

Do you not think it rather pretty, little reader, that a very part of the flower which has spent so long a time in one unchanging place should at last go free into the world—a tiny being filled with sleeping life—ready to burst forth at the given moment into a new and beautiful plant the same as that from which it itself has come?

WILD PARSLEY

(LOMATIA—type silaifolia)

Family: Proteaceae.

Flowering season: Summer, but sometimes even winter.

Flowers: Cream coloured, with four petals, four stamens joined to the petals and a curved style. Before the petals fall off they become separated from one another. The flowers are arranged in pairs up the stem.

Leaves: Much divided and of firm texture.

Seeds: Winged. The fruit is a black-coloured box. Between the seeds, a yellow-coloured dust can be seen.

The Story of the Tall Greenhood Fairy

(PTEROSTYLIS—type longifolia)

Just the same as humans have proper as well as nicknames, we flowers have them too; and so it is that although I am formally called Pterostylis, I am affectionately called Greenhood. I must admit that Greenhood sounds prettier and more homely; but all the same, I wish I could hear my other name too, more often, because then, you see I would know that mortals were taking a keener interest in me.

That large bonnet which I always wear, and those long, fine feelers are rather pretty, don't you think? I simply love you to take notice of them, for naturally, flowers long to be loved by everyone. But I feel very particularly happy if the musical mosquitoes admire them, for I can never be quite sure of humans, but mosquitoes are always kind to me. Of course, they have no idea they are being kind; but please do not tell them I said so, because they may get awfully offended and not come near me any more. One learns from experience that mosquitoes are funny things to deal with, and inclined to become somewhat peeved if flowers do not appreciate them thoroughly.

As well as my prettily coloured flowers, I also keep something else which I am sure will tempt them to visit me. It is a sort of sweet-tasting liquid—and if you have ever entered into an intimate conversation with a mosquito, you will already know how fond he is of being entertained with a little something to eat and drink.

Well, the smallest one of my petals is what many people call my "tongue," and this petal is very, very sensitive; so that when the tiny visitor comes along and steps upon it even as gently as can be, it suddenly springs up from its hanging-down position, thus holding him entrapped—but not quite! There is still a tiny open passage through which he can escape; and I have taken the greatest care that in retreating by this one and only outlet, he must brush past my ripe pollen bags, which quickly shake off some of their fine yellow dust right over that funny little hump on his back.

Now he flies away, singing and buzzing in sheer joy at having regained his freedom. And then, so that he may enjoy his adventure again, he makes his way to another Orchid the same as I, and walks straight in. But, as he does so, he passes by the very sticky stigma where, of course, some of the pollen gets caught—and only then has it reached its destination.

As you can see, this saves me a great deal of trouble, for no flowers can

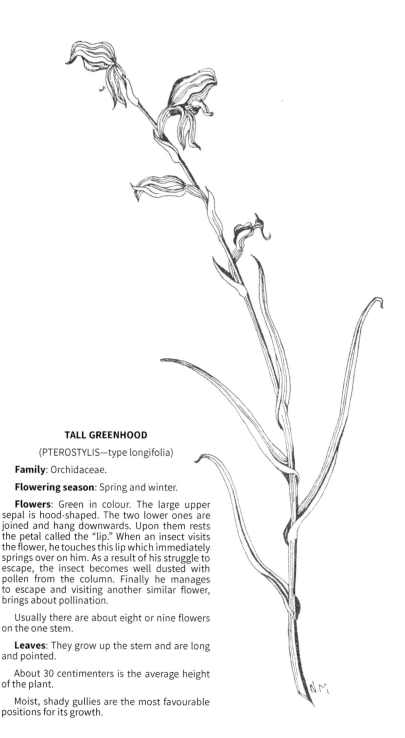

TALL GREENHOOD

(PTEROSTYLIS—type longifolia)

Family: Orchidaceae.

Flowering season: Spring and winter.

Flowers: Green in colour. The large upper sepal is hood-shaped. The two lower ones are joined and hang downwards. Upon them rests the petal called the "lip." When an insect visits the flower, he touches this lip which immediately springs over on him. As a result of his struggle to escape, the insect becomes well dusted with pollen from the column. Finally he manages to escape and visiting another similar flower, brings about pollination.

Usually there are about eight or nine flowers on the one stem.

Leaves: They grow up the stem and are long and pointed.

About 30 centimenters is the average height of the plant.

Moist, shady gullies are the most favourable positions for its growth.

grow into more flowers unless their pollen is carried from one to the other. If Mr. Mosquito did not oblige me, just think of the terrible amount of walking about I would have to do!

And now, little mortal child, if you have grown to love me as I love you, please come and visit me whenever you can. My address is:

Amongst mosses and maiden-hair,

Fern-strewn gullies.

And the date of my appearance is winter and spring.

Mosquitoes like to be entertained.

The Wattle Fairy

(ACACIA—type longifolia, variety typica)

Often I think that the members of family Wattle (which are very numerous indeed—far more so than those of any human family) are similar to mortals in at least one respect: in that there are short, round Wattles, long, thin ones, short, thin ones, and long, fat ones. In other words, there is every possible shape of Wattle, just the same as there is every possible shape of human. Although (I may be biased in this) I always think that Wattles possess a stronger claim to elegance than do humans.

Well, of all these kinds, I am a long and fat one, and as I am to be found quite plentifully in many places, I am sure you must have seen and picked me often. I hope that when you pass by me next time, along some bush-track, you will lean over and whisper something in my ear about my being pretty to look at. Now, you may think me vain, and perhaps you think rightly, but I have to admit that with nearly all flowers, vanity is a very common fault.

Have you ever looked at my leaves closely, little human? I wonder. If you have, you will have noticed how long and flat they are. Yet in reality—and here is the funny part of it—they are not leaves at all, but flattened stems. You see, Australia is rather a hot, dry country to live in; and the sun, although he is responsible for our continued lives, can also be very cruel, and can steal from us with his heat the water which we drink from the earth and which saves us from dying of thirst and hunger.

So that, it would be an easy thing for us just to die away and be forgotten. But, dear Mother Nature, who is so gentle and so wise, could never allow anything like that to happen. And that is why she has flattened out my stems for me, making them look like leaves. For stems are generally more careful, and are able to store valuable food that leaves would simply give over to Father Sun with very little more than a word.

I suppose you have often heard it said that the Wattle is the national flower of Australia; and in case you do not know why this should be, I shall tell you straight away. It is because, out of the five hundred members of my family, three hundred live in Australia, and only two hundred have chosen to go abroad. How would you like to have four hundred and nine-nine brothers and sisters, as I have? I can assure you it is very interesting— you see, I can claim relationship to so many of the flowers in Bushland. But remembering all their names is not quite so pleasant—especially as they are always ready to accuse me of neglect if I mix them up a bit.

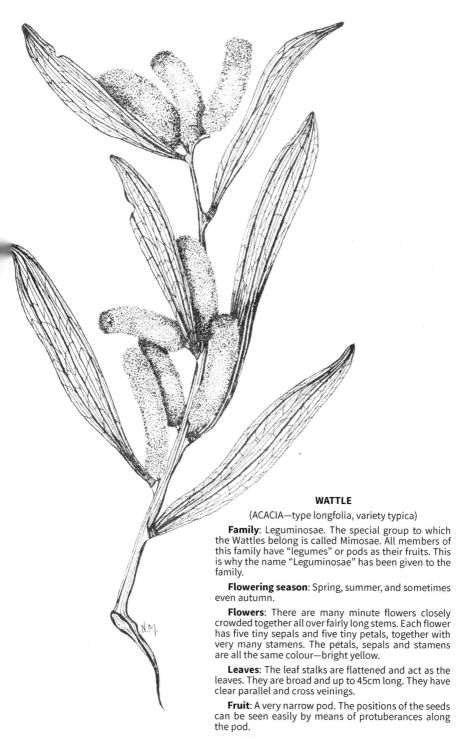

WATTLE

(ACACIA—type longfolia, variety typica)

Family: Leguminosae. The special group to which the Wattles belong is called Mimosae. All members of this family have "legumes" or pods as their fruits. This is why the name "Leguminosae" has been given to the family.

Flowering season: Spring, summer, and sometimes even autumn.

Flowers: There are many minute flowers closely crowded together all over fairly long stems. Each flower has five tiny sepals and five tiny petals, together with very many stamens. The petals, sepals and stamens are all the same colour—bright yellow.

Leaves: The leaf stalks are flattened and act as the leaves. They are broad and up to 45cm long. They have clear parallel and cross veinings.

Fruit: A very narrow pod. The positions of the seeds can be seen easily by means of protuberances along the pod.

35

Then there are those two hundred in other parts of the world (mostly in the tropics of the Southern Hemisphere)—they are another problem. I wish they would all come over to Australia, and make correspondence a little less difficult. Sometimes years go by, and I do not hear from one of them, and not one of them hears from me.

But we are really a very happy family. In fact, our soft, pretty flowers (varying in colour from pure white to deep yellow) are so abundant and make our bushes look so bright, that, amongst humans, they seem to be actual symbols of happiness.

Oh, golden are the gumleaves as the zephyrs o'er them blow,
And golden is the sunny light that makes them shimmer so.
And Autumn colours other leaves with hues so wondrous bold
That when they fall, they spread the earth with canopies of gold!

The little wand'ring buttercup that haunts the riverside
Is brilliant gold—and in her heart the golden nectar hides.
The azure heavens golden turn when lit with sunset glow;
And golden are my stamens a-swaying to and fro!

My pollen dust is golden-hued, which in my flower I hold,
And insects, when they brush me by, are also dusted gold.
I love to see the woodlands, with all my shrubs in bloom,
Transformed to Springtide's golden life from Winter's misty gloom!

" . . . . each beauteous flower,
Iris all hues, roses, and jessamine
Reared high their flourished heads between, and wrought
Mosaic; underfoot the violet,
Crocus, and hyacinth, with rich inlay
Broidered the ground, more coloured than with stone
Of costliest emblem."

—Milton.

The Waratah Fairy
(TELOPEA—type speciosissima)

The shy Wild Violet, drooping her head over a woodland stream, says sadly to me: "Ah, you are a bold and hardened flower. You are so sure of your great beauty that there is no sweet timidity in you."

The dainty Bluebell nods to and fro as she chimes in: "Yes, you are haughty indeed, and have no time to talk with your little companions who have not grown as tall and majestic as you."

Then says the wicked Mountain Devil: "There is no mischief in your eye; there is no impishness in your ways. You are always cold and reserved, and give me a disdainful glance every time I prick or make faces at anyone. I do not, I cannot, I will not, like you!" And with this, his wrathful bush shakes so much and stamps its roots so peevishly into the earth, that all the lovely red flowers fall off, and very soon the shrub is covered with dozens of little devil-heads.

Now, you may think that all this abuse makes my life one long misery. But there you are mistaken, for it amuses me ever so much and helps to bring a little variety into my life.

But I do not only **hear** these remarks; sometimes I actually manage to bend my very stiff neck just enough to see the speakers. When they notice that I am looking at them closely, they usually feel a bit ashamed of themselves. The little Violet is very sweet and, having smiled at me, as much as to say: "Do not misunderstand me, Sir Waratah; I was really only teasing, and right inside me I am truly fond of you," and she fixes her eyes upon her image in the stream. Young Bluebell tries to pretend that nothing whatsoever had been said, and that my inspection had not been noticed, by giving voice to a long chorus of "Ding dong, ding dong, ding dong bell" without even glancing in my direction.

Also, it happens at times that when Mountain Devil, in a spasm of extra peevishness, buries four or five of his sharply-pointed leaves into my stalk, I look down suddenly at him with a frown. Of course, his guilty conscience tells him that my face is fiery red with anger; the result being that I do not hear or feel anything else from him for quite a long time—perhaps even ten minutes.

However, I am not angry, for I must admit that I have a very even temper, being mostly that "cool, calm and collected" type.

WARATAH

(TELOPEA—type speciosissima)

Family: Proteaceae. This family has been named after the sea-god Proteus, who was able to change his form at will, because of the great differences to be seen in the leaves, flowers and fruits of its many members.

Flowering season: spring.

Flowers: Red in colour. The large head consists of many flowers, arranged in pairs on the end of the stem. There are four petals, united to form a tube. In this tube there is a slit through which the pistil comes. There are four stamens, one attached to the tip of each petal. When the pollen is ripe, the tips of the petals roll back and the pistil springs to an upright position. Many large bracts surround the head and help to protect it. Each flower has a great deal of honey which attracts insects and birds to it. The Honeysucker is a usual visitor, his long beak easily reaching the end of the tube. While doing so, his feathers get dusted with pollen, which he unconsciously leaves on the pistil of the next Waratah flower he visits.

Leaves: From 12 to 25cm in length, the leaves are dark green in colour and oblong. Like Gum leaves, they are often found turned in such a way that only their edges face the sun directly. As very much water is lost from the surface of the leaf (when the sun is very hot) it can be seen that this twisting protects the surface from the direct heat of the sun and so lessens the amount of water lost from the plant.

Fruit: A long pod, which splits open on one side and sets free many seeds, each of which has a long wing attached to it.

The flowers who grow only to a small height think my existence must be wearisome and uninteresting, away up in the air. But, of course, they are quite wrong, for I have the loveliest friends imaginable. I am nearer to the Lillipilly than they are, and to the Christmas Bush and Wattle and Gum and ever so many others. These are my friends, and we have the most enlightening conversations at times about the sunshine and the storm clouds, the winds and the rains.

Then also, there is Mr. Honeysucker, who is extremely amiable, and who brings us news from all over Bushland. He is far more interesting, I am sure, than any of the newspapers which mortals leave around us sometimes. These seem concerned only with armies and navies and the making of machine guns. But Mr. Honeysucker tells us of the amazing industry of ants, which enables them to build immense homes for themselves so quickly. He relates to us the doings of the famous Blue wren family that lives in such a tree round such a bend in the bush track leading to such a place—and of Billy the Bullfinch and Christopher the Kingfisher. News of this description is, it seems to me, far more profitable than any of quarrels and wars.

You must already know me very well, little human, so there is hardly need for me to describe myself. You must not think for a moment, however, that my large crimson head is only one flower; for it is very many flowers all crowded together, the top ones of which are "slow-coaches" and are still to be found in bud when the lower ones have unfolded into blooms. Unlike most flowers, mine have no sepals. Now, as you know, it is the duty of sepals to protect the flower and hold it firmly together; so that when they are not present, some other way of protecting must be thought out. In my case, you will see that there are a great many red leaves called "bracts" surrounding my large group of flowers. These protect them while they are all tiny buds, and afterwards help to keep them safely attached to the stem to which they cling as tightly as they can. I am afraid, however, they would fall off easily, if it were not for the kind persistence of those bracts.

I can feel that cheeky Mountain Devil pricking me again. He is telling me I have been talking far too much, and had better stop straight away. So I shall take his advice as soon as I have sung my little song to you.

They call me proud and haughty
And arrogant and bold;
They say I am by nature
Intolerably cold.

But they are only teasing,
And in my heart I know
They'd sadly weep if ever
I went elsewhere to grow—

For often I have heard them
(When I have been so still
That they have thought me sleeping)
With admiration fill.

They've praised my height and grandeur,
And e'en my haughty stand.
They've said how proud to own me
Must be our sunny land.

I smile—But no-one sees me—
And gaily wink my eye,
Then innocently fix it
Upon the azure sky!

The Flannel Flower Fairy

(ACTINOTUS—type Helianthi)

It often amuses us flowers very much to hear the opinions that some mortals have of us. Of course, botanists are different, as they spend a great deal of their time studying us, and so are well acquainted with us and our habits.

But it always sounds very funny to us when people talk about the Arum Lily (which in reality is no lily at all) and the Asparagus Fern (which has nothing to do with a fern) and the petals of a Sunflower (which are not petals at all, but certain kinds of leaves called bracts) and again, the petals of the Flannel Flower, which are also just bracts. Then, there are many humans who think of me as belonging to the same family as the Daisy, whereas in reality, the Daisy's family (Compositae by name) and mine (Umbelliferae) are entirely different from one another.

Now, I suppose you will ask why it is that there are some flowers—both wild and cultivated—which are provided with these pretty, decorative bracts, whilst there are so many which haven't them at all. Well, I think you will be able to answer that question for yourselves if you try to imagine what a Daisy or a Zinnia or a Poinsettia or a Sunflower or a Flannel Flower would look like without its many bracts. In each case you will see how very unattractive those "centres" would appear if left all alone. And now, if you look carefully enough, you will see that what you had thought of merely as a part of one flower, is really many flowers all crowded together as closely as can be, forming what you call the "centre."

Of course, each little bloom is extremely small, so its petals are also very tiny and, to the casual observer, not important in the least. Neither are they noticeable to bees and other insects. And that is why those certain kind leaves named bracts have come to our assistance, making us visible to everyone. What we would do without them, I really do not know. I think we would be the most neglected flowers in the whole world, for we would never be visited by insects or admired by humans.

I think that my little readers all know why they call me a Flannel Flower, because they must all have seen me at least once or twice so far, and felt the soft woolliness of every part of me— from my green-tipped white bracts to my stems and leaves.

You see, just like the Wattle, who has already told you her story, and like very, very many other wildflowers, I have made my home not in gullies, but on the dry, rather barren hills, where there is little protection from the sun's rays. And as my Wattle friend has explained to you, sunbeams can be cruel as well as kind, and can steal from us the clear, cool water that thoughtful rains have given us to drink. That is why you will find a thick coat of wax on gum leaves, which does not allow the water to escape from them, and a thick woollen coat on my leaves, which not only protects them from the hear of sunbeams, but also from the hard, dry winds.

FLANNEL FLOWER.

(ACINOTUS—type helianthi)

Family: Umbelliferae. This name is given beacause the members of the family have their flowers arranged like the ribs of an umbrella.

Flowering seasons: Spring and summer.

Flowers: Very minute, and arranged like the ribs of an umbrella. They are surrounded by large white leaves (called "bracts") which are tipped with green. The outer flowers have no pistil—only five stamens. The inner ones have a pistil, which has two tubes called styles which

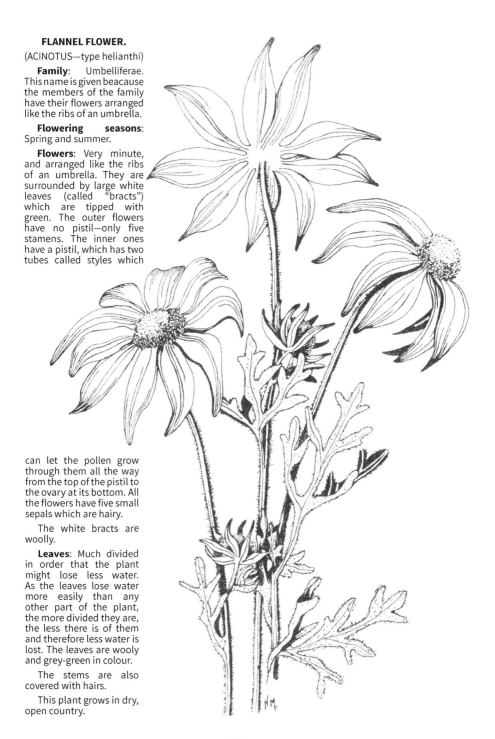

can let the pollen grow through them all the way from the top of the pistil to the ovary at its bottom. All the flowers have five small sepals which are hairy.

The white bracts are woolly.

Leaves: Much divided in order that the plant might lose less water. As the leaves lose water more easily than any other part of the plant, the more divided they are, the less there is of them and therefore less water is lost. The leaves are wooly and grey-green in colour.

The stems are also covered with hairs.

This plant grows in dry, open country.

43

The Song of the Leopard Fairy

(DIURIS—type maculata)

I am such a fairy Orchid! Yes, of course, we all are! But some of my brothers and sisters and cousins become so much changed in the daytime from what they look like as fairies at midnight, that you really cannot think that they ever were fairies— but you only have to glance at me to see that I'm a fairy.

Just look how I cross my dainty legs and dance all day to the songs of birds and the buzz of bees and the rustling of grass— mortals would call them sepals; my brothers and sisters and aunts and uncles and cousins would call them sepals, but I am such a fairy Orchid, I must call them legs. Oh, I can't stop singing, I can't stop dancing, and this is the song I sing all day:

> Brilliant gold with freckles brown,
>> Open lands I love to grace:
> Shady nooks would not allow
>> Sunny beams to seek my face.
>
> 'Midst the grasses tall I hide;
>> Humans' love I seldom hold,
> Yet my little flowers are formed
>> Out of Nature's purest gold.
>
> Frilly skirt and twinkle feet,
>> I upon the zephyrs dance
> By the roadside all the day
>> In a dreamy, fairy trance.
>
> By the roadside, on the hills,
>> Just a blossom in the light—
> When the world in silence sleeps,
>> Lovely fairy of the night!

LEOPARD ORCHID

(DIURIS—type maculata)

Family: Orchidaceae.

Flowering season: spring.

Flowers: Yellow in colour, usually much marked with brown. The lip (largest petal) is three-lobed. The two long, narrow, lower sepals cross each other. There are many different kinds of Diuris, and in plenty of them this crossing of the two lower sepals is seen.

There are usually from two to ten flowers on one stalk.

Leaves: Long, narrow and grass-like.

The Story of Little Blue Lobelia

(LOBELIA—type gibbosa)

(Told by MR. HONEYSUCKER)

Little Lobelia gibbosa was on the verge of jumping up and speaking to you this minute, but I, just a young Honeysucker, have flown along instead; and I have done this for the simple reason that I am so interested in this particular wildflower fairy.

As you can see by the name that people call me, I spend almost the whole of my life searching for honey. That is why I visit so many of the wildflowers which grow in Australia; for, you see, some of them are simply filled with honey. And, unless you have tasted it yourself, little human—unless you have actually sipped it, syrupy and sweet, from the very flowers in which it has been formed—I am sure you could never understand how delicious it is, or how I long for **more** as soon as I have tasted **some**, or how I devote my life to the finding of it.

But I am wandering away somewhat from the things I want to tell you.

In all my searches through plainlands, mountains and gullies, I do not remember ever having met a flower quite as fascinating as Lobelia. Of course, each one of them is very lovely in its own way, and I am fond of every one separately. Bur I suppose we must all have favourites. And so it is that every time I meet Lobelia I feel extra-specially happy.

At the magic hour, when I become a fairy bird I meet her as a fairy flower, and we walk and talk together a great deal, until the sky begins to put away its starry jewels and cast aside its heavy cloak of darkness. And because of this I have grown to know much more about her than the cleverest of humans do— although I am afraid I still know very little.

Lobelia is not as attractive to look at as are some of the other bush flowers. At the most, her plant is only about sixty centimeters high.

Her leaves are small, and not particularly graceful. Her flowers are also small and perhaps not very noticeable to unobservant eyes. But they are the colour of the sky at midnight, and to me they appear very lovely indeed. So much so, in fact, that whenever I see them, I cannot possibly resist them.

And the nearer I fly down to them, the more certain I begin to feel that there is a vast supply of honey awaiting me. Oh, how excited I grow then!

LOBELIA
(LOBELIA—type GIBBOSA)

Family: Campanulaceae. This family receives its name from a latin word meaning "bell." This is because so many of the flowers belonging to it are shaped like bells.

Flowering season: summer.

Flowers: Dark blue in colour. Five purplish sepals partly joined. Five petals which are not all the same in shape, and the bases of which are joined to form a small tube. The two upper ones are small, and curved backwards; the three lower ones are large and outspread, the middle one having three white lines on it which lead to the honey store. The flat blue stalks of the stamens serve to protect the honey, and the blue anthers form a tube which ends with tufts of hairs. The pistil's tubular 'style' also ends in hairs, and the stigma consists of two blue lobes.

Leaves: Not all alike in shape. The lower ones are wide and toothed; the upper ones narrow, and seldom toothed.

And how rapidly I continue my journey, until I am actually hovering about those dark blue flowers themselves.

But here is the puzzling part of the whole affair: it seems as if Lobelia, through a certain kind of perverseness that some flowers enjoy, is at the same time anxious and unwilling to entertain me. Of course, I know that she keeps her store of honey well concealed with those blue stamens of hers, so that it will not be stolen by the many insects who would like to run away with it. But all the same, it does seem rather bad behaviour towards me (an old friend) and at first I become considerably peeved.

I soon forget my troubles, however, when I find that in reality she is quite friendly towards me, and has done all she could to help me. For, upon her largest petal and leading to her precious honey store, there are three of the finest white lines. Now, for some unknown reason, I know what they mean and where they lead to, whereas all other birds and the great majority of insects never have the slightest idea of either. That is why there is always plenty of honey for me to enjoy. And you can be sure I do enjoy it.

I then say "thank you" and "good-bye" to the little blue flower. But as I do so, it happens without exception that I find on my feathers a tiny sprinkling of fine, yellow dust (which humans call "pollen," I believe). I look at it for a moment and wonder what it all means. The only thing I can be sure of is that Lobelia sprinkled it on me while I was busy a-honeying.

But after much wondering, I finally come to this decision: That it is a message of some kind that Lobelia wanted to send to one of her kinsfolk somewhere else in Bushland; and that she had treated me to particularly sweet honey so that I would be tempted to seek out another flower exactly like her, as soon as I had left her. Then, naturally, I would deliver the secret message when I had found the other, and all would be well.

What the message itself contains, however, I never can find out, although I guess and wonder about it a great deal. Perhaps it is an invitation to a Lobelia ball. Perhaps it is merely a piece of wildflower gossip. And perhaps it is a little message of love.

There is a flood of all-melodious songs,
A ceaseless harmony, and heaven's calm
That breathes upon my brow an airy charm;
A bubbling brook within which flowery throngs
Their beauty wistfully admire—and wrongs
Of men so far from this immortal balm
Of bushland peace appear. Each threat'ning harm,
 Here melts to naught, where God's own power belongs.

The Fairy of the Hilltops

(SPRENGELIA—type incarnata)

On the hilltops where the winds blow fiercely and where the grass is crisp and brown—that is where I grow, holding up staunchly my clusters of pale pink flowers and my long, stiff stems, covered all over by the sharply-pointed leaves that fold around them.

In springtime, when the birds sing sweetly and when dainty butterflies dance hither and thither, showing to the open plainlands their colourful wings, and carelessly sipping honey from all the flowers in turn, life is a happy and beautiful thing indeed.

But sometimes I unfold my petals before the warm spring comes, in the bleak winter. And then—Oh, the winds are fierce and destructive, the rains are speeding and cold, the sky is dark and dreary, and the hilltops are sad, for

> There is no butterfly, no bird,
> No sunshine warm and bright,
> No melody that Summer heard,
> Upon the mountain height.
>
> The angry storm clouds sweeping by
> O'ershade the hillsides steep,
> And rush upon their wild, dark course,
> Then sorrowfully weep!

SPRENGELIA—type incarnata

Family: Epacridaceae. To this family also belong the Heaths.

Flowering season: Spring, but sometimes even winter.

Flowers: Pale pink in colour and much crowded together. Five long, narrow petals. Five long, narrow, white sepals. There is a short corolla tube. The anthers are long and form a ring round the short pistil.

Leaves: Much crowded. Their bases fold round the stem, and each ends with a long, sharp point.

51

The Spurred Helmet Fairy

(CORYSANTHES—type aconitiflorus)

They call me a tiny helmet—
Ah yes, it is very true;
But there's something more than a helmet
About me, I think, don't you?

Oh, see me, a warrior fierce and bold,
With a sharp little sparkling eye,
And a most professional soldier's frown
And a shrill little soldier's cry!

Yes, though I am small, I have a very keen expression and character, as all my life, from the earliest moment I can remember, I have been a brave soldier, and it is because I used always to be crouching down in pursuit of the enemy that I simply got the habit, and at the present time no matter how straight I stand I am still quite tiny. But of course I don't mind, as I know my noble height has been sacrificed to nothing but kindness; for you know whom I mean by the "enemy," don't you? Why, caterpillars, snails, and all those tiny insects which creep into us and steal our honey without doing us the favour of carrying away some of our pollen in return. They give us a tremendous amount of extra work to do, making new honey to tempt the mosquitoes, beetles and birds, who are not nearly as selfish. So you can imagine how we long to be strong enough to chase them right away.

Day after day I stand on duty, adorned by my brilliant helmet, waiting for an opportunity to attack; thus you can see how it is I have such a sunburnt appearance—even my helmet has gone a rusty sort of purple colour, whilst my only leaf, which is, indeed, larger than I and which is my constant companion, is not a fresh, clear green, but has become tinged with a dull mixture of purple, crimson, brown and yellow.

I suppose it is because this helmet of mine is so large when compared with the rest of me that people think I am nothing except it, and, would you believe it, they just tread right on top of me sometimes because they do not see me at all. Of course, I could hardly expect anything else, I suppose, when my plant consists of a tiny root, a big leaf, a short stem and a flower.

A long, long time ago when I was tall and commanding, I often used to ride a big, black horse at midnight and wear glittering spurs on my boots; but now I am so tubby, I think I may just roll off if I attempted to mount a horse again, so I stay safely on the ground all the time, mostly with my feet in dark, rich soil at the bottom of trees; but, can you guess what I have done?

SPURRED HELMET ORCHID.
(CORYSANTHES—type aconitiflorus)

Family: Orchidaceae.

Flowering season: winter.

Flowers: Purplish in colour. The largest sepal is shaped like a hood and ends at the base with two spurs.

Leaf: Lies flat on the ground, is roughly rounded in shape and large in comparison with the flower. Its colour is usually dark and purplish.

The whole plant is very small and short.

Well, I have fastened my spurs upon my helmet, partly to make it prettier, and partly to remind me of my glorious past.

Although I am very fond of my Orchid friends I have grown a little fearful these last few thousand years or so of getting crushed by mistake amongst the tremendous crowd of them which gathers together at spring-time, so I quietly open out my flower while they are still fast asleep beneath the ground, waiting for the warmer weather to come, and then I sink down just as quietly again into Mother Earth as they are opening out their little shoots and looking about them.

> They call me a tiny helmet—
> Ah yes, it is very true;
> But there's something more than a helmet
> About me, I think, don't you?

In pursuit of the enemy.

The Wild Flower Traveller

(CLEMATIS—type aristata)

They call me a trav'ller in Bushland—
The fairies and elfins and gnomes.
They look at me wand'ring the hillside
And say: "We have comfortable homes
Which we love and we prize and we care for,
While yonder white flower only roams!"

They speak of my habits with pity;
They watch as I come and I go;
They say that the pleasures of home-life
I "never—oh, never, could know."
They ask why I cannot be flower-like,
And settle in one place to grow?

But **I** love the call of adventure,
Its sound is like music to me.
I hear it, and then I must follow,
Wherever its dwelling may be—
Perhaps over large, frowning boulders,
Perhaps at the top of a tree.

Yet ne'er does my spirit grow older.
Through winter and summer I cling
Alike, and the forests I travel:
For autumn and winter **do** bring
A fluffy, grey beard to my features—
But blossoms return with the spring.

Oh, grand are those calls of adventure,
(Which many a flower cannot hear)
And grand is the spirit of roving
Whose song is so wild and so clear!
How could I regret that its music
Sounds ever more sweet in my ear?

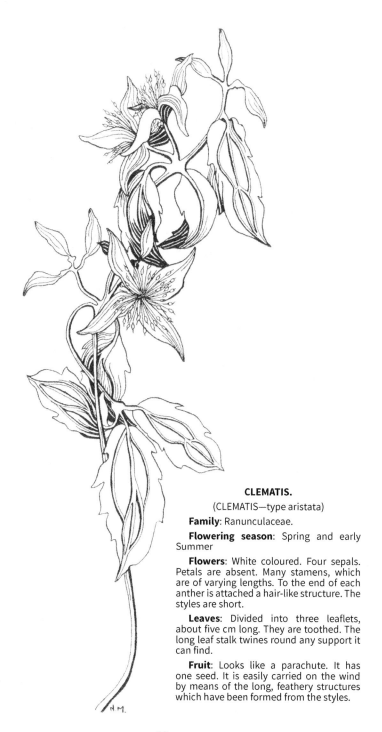

CLEMATIS.

(CLEMATIS—type aristata)

Family: Ranunculaceae.

Flowering season: Spring and early Summer

Flowers: White coloured. Four sepals. Petals are absent. Many stamens, which are of varying lengths. To the end of each anther is attached a hair-like structure. The styles are short.

Leaves: Divided into three leaflets, about five cm long. They are toothed. The long leaf stalk twines round any support it can find.

Fruit: Looks like a parachute. It has one seed. It is easily carried on the wind by means of the long, feathery structures which have been formed from the styles.

57

The Heathy Parrot Pea Fairy

(DILLWYNIA—type ericifolia)

I have not always been a flower, you know—in fact, very few flowers have been, from the beginning of time, what they are now. Many thousands of centuries ago, I used to dance about the world on tip-toes as the prettiest butterfly you could imagine. My wings were not very large, nor even fancifully formed (as those of some butterflies are) but their colour was so bright that it was almost dazzling, and made them look just like pieces of the sky at sunset. Sometimes they were brilliant yellow, other times a rich orange. But always they were marked here and there with a deep, beautiful red.

The elves and fairies, of course, used to love me very much, and I used to love them. For one happy day we would frolic amongst the trees and ferns, then flutter up into the sky together; and when we began to feel a little hungry, we would all come down again and take a tiny sip of honey from the prettiest flower we could find.

But alas! At the end of that day which had been filled to the brim with joy and laughter, I would become so weary that I could not even smile at my fairy companions, and very soon my wings would fold gently around me, and I would die.

Now, this used to be a great sorrow to me, for life was so sweet and the sunshine so happy, and the whole wide world so beautiful.

Oh! how I used to think and think, as hard as I could, wondering what I might do to live just a little longer. The fairies thought, also; and the funny wee elves, putting on their considering caps, could only ever rest their chins in their hands and make wry faces, wrinkling their foreheads and screwing up their noses.

It was a sad problem indeed, and none of us, with all our efforts, could solve it. Then one day, as we were flying through the woods, we heard a very small, tearful voice. It seemed to come from somewhere near us, so we stopped suddenly and looked around for the speaker, hoping to bring it some comfort. And we did not take long in finding it, either, for it was quite a tall bush standing right beside us. Its leaves were rather small, fine and prickly. It had many long branches which drooped ever so slightly—and altogether it was a dainty little bush, which I immediately began to love.

"Oh," it cried plaintively, "I am sad and neglected. Every other plant around me is covered with sweet flowers which make it look so colourful

HEATHY PARROT PEA.

(DILLWYNIA—type ericifolia)

Family: Leguminosae. The group to which this flower belongs is called Papilionaceae, which comes from a Latin word meaning "butterfly." The group was given this name because of the likeness which its various flowers bear to the outspread wings of butterflies.

Flowering season: Spring and summer.

Flowers: They grow in loose clusters near the ends of branches, and are often orange-coloured with red markings. The largest petal is called the "standard." The two side ones are called the "wings," and the two small front ones, which are partly joined together, the "keel."

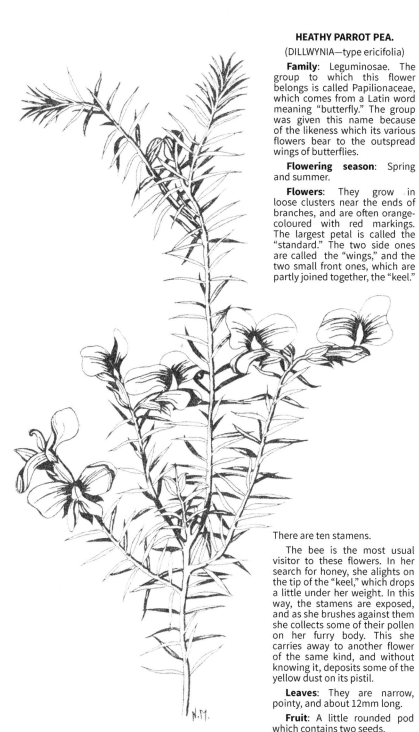

There are ten stamens.

The bee is the most usual visitor to these flowers. In her search for honey, she alights on the tip of the "keel," which drops a little under her weight. In this way, the stamens are exposed, and as she brushes against them she collects some of their pollen on her furry body. This she carries away to another flower of the same kind, and without knowing it, deposits some of the yellow dust on its pistil.

Leaves: They are narrow, pointy, and about 12mm long.

Fruit: A little rounded pod which contains two seeds.

and gay; yet I have only stems and leaves. I do believe I am the only shrub in this big world without a flower upon it. Can nobody give me a flower for my very own, to keep and be proud of always?"

Immediately I heard these words, I knew that my opportunity had come, and that my life need never again last only for one short day. Quickly, I fluttered my way to the top of the longest branch, and there I nestled in amongst the small, green leaves— and became a flower!

The little bush nearly cried for joy—but it was no happier than I. "Look," it said excitedly to its companions, "I have a butterfly for a flower—a butterfly who is beloved of the fairies!"

And ever since then, I have heard mortals remark on the likeness I bear to the little winged creatures that often dance around me. Yet they never seem to realise the full extent of that likeness between us, or the fact that although I have the petals of a flower I have the soul of a butterfly.

Some people, referring to my colours, call me "Eggs and Bacon." Well, perhaps there is something in that too, although I cannot say I am very fond of it—and besides, that is really the popular name of one of my brothers,* whose petals are yellow for the most part with only the tiniest bit of red in them. The leaves of that plant are much closer together than mine, and the flowers are in more definite clusters. Also, it is a shorter shrub than I am, often not growing to any height worthy of mention.

> And so, a flower forever more
> I shall remain, and ever grow
> Where all day long the sun's bright rays
> Will round me glow!
>
> For it was by a craving strong
> That I became a little flower—
> And real desire within the heart
> Has magic power!

*DILLWYNIA floribunda.

"I've watched you now a full half-hour;
Self-poised upon that yellow flower
And, little Butterfly! indeed
I know not if you sleep or feed.
          . . . .
This plot of orchard-ground is ours;
    My trees they are, my Sister's flowers,
Here rest your wings when they are weary;
Here lodge as in a sanctuary!
Come often to us, fear no wrong;
Sit near us on the bough!
We'll talk of sunshine and of song,
And summer days, when we were young;
    Sweet, childish days, that were as long
As twenty days are now."

—Wordsworth.

The Red Spider Flower Fairy

(GREVILLEA—type punicea)

Although people seem to think that my long, spreading red flowers look most attractive and are a great asset to the Australian bush, I do believe I am even more proud of the distinguished family to which I belong than of any flattering remark that I hear about myself personally.

Just the same as human families have names, so flower families have them also—and some of them look for all the world like Double Dutch. But mine is Proteaceae, which isn't bad at all.

You will see why I have called it a "distinguished" family when you know that only a few of its members are: the Waratahs, the Mountain Devils, the Parsley Plants, the beautiful Flame Wheel Tree of Queensland, the Bottlebrushes, and all the Grevilleas.

Now "Grevillea" is one of my names. But as I have to share it with a hundred and fifty-five other members of family Proteaceae, "punicea" has also been given to me. And that one name, at least, is exclusively mine.

We Grevilleas are a very hardy race; and some of us are ever so pretty, particularly Grevillea Banksii, who lives in Queensland. Some, naturally, are more delicate than others. But we have adapted ourselves to such varied conditions that you will find species of us growing in the sandy desert in the middle of this continent just as easily as others are able to grow in damper regions round the coast.

So that all together, I think you can now imagine what a fairyland of wonder it would be if every member of family Proteaceae could be encouraged to flower at the same time and in the same garden. Perhaps some day a kind magician or a fairy with a magic wand will make it possible. And then, I can almost see the throngs of people coming from far and wide to witness the fanciful sight.

It seems rather out of place now to talk about myself—so unimportant a unit of a glorious whole—does it not? But I think perhaps you would be interested to know that the under side of my leaves is covered with either silvery or bronze-coloured hairs which make them look very pretty.

Next time you are in the bush—no matter at what season of the year, for I flower nearly always—if you happen to pass my way and think you recognise me, you won't forget to look for those tiny hairs, will you? And if you do not find them—well, you will know you have come across one of my brother or sister Grevilleas instead.

RED SPIDER FLOWER.

(GREVILLEA—type punicea)

Family: Proteaceae.

Flowering season: Throughout the whole year.

Flowers: Red in colour, produced very close together in fairly large numbers, and arranged in pairs. Four united petals. The tube formed by these united petals is hairy inside. The four stamens, joined to the petals, are borne on the free petal lobes. The style is long, and the stigma is only released from the corolla tube when the pollen is mature.

Leaves: Oblong and about 4cm long. The underside is covered with bronze or silver coloured hairs.

Fruit: Pod-like, containing two seeds, and about 12mm long.

63

The Lament of the Spider Orchid

(CALADENIA—type Patersonii)

I used to be an ogre
In a great, ferocious cavern;
I used to trap the butterflies,
I used to eat the dragonflies,
I caught the fairies by surprise,
And Puck and Jack-o'-Lantern!

Once upon a time I was
The giant of all the spiders.
I used to prowl the woods by night
And carry elfins off in fright—
Oh, how they scattered at the sight
Of me—the giant of spiders!

But then there came a hero
With a white and sweeping feather!
He said he was a fairy knight,
We had a long and mighty fight,
And when I was defeated quite
He said to me in accent slight:
"What very pleasant weather!"

Then, waving over me his wand,
Declared: "You heartless midnight glider!
You'll be a flower forever more—
No longer fairies frighten, for
You're nothing greater after all
Than what the whole wide world will call
An 'artificial spider'!"

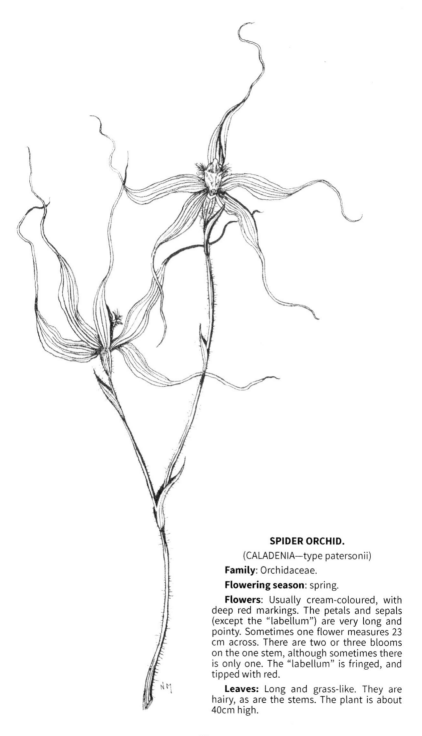

SPIDER ORCHID.

(CALADENIA—type patersonii)

Family: Orchidaceae.

Flowering season: spring.

Flowers: Usually cream-coloured, with deep red markings. The petals and sepals (except the "labellum") are very long and pointy. Sometimes one flower measures 23 cm across. There are two or three blooms on the one stem, although sometimes there is only one. The "labellum" is fringed, and tipped with red.

Leaves: Long and grass-like. They are hairy, as are the stems. The plant is about 40cm high.

The Dwarf Apple Fairy

(ANGOPHORA—type cordifolia)

Looking at my large, full clusters of creamish-coloured flowers, you could easily imagine me to be a gum tree. But the fact that when quite grown-up I am still only a shrub would make you think otherwise. And together with this difference between us there are many more—for instance, gum leaves are smooth and are sometimes (especially when young) shiny. But my leaves have rather a dull appearance always, and the baby ones are covered with a thick coat of hairs. Then also, they are arranged in pairs opposite to one another along my stems, whereas those of the gum trees are not.

The leaves of a very near relation of mine* are more similar to the Eucalyptus, being long and ending with a point. But mine are short, and rounded at the tip.

Even in the flowers themselves there are differences to be found. You all know quite well the little lid which covers the gum blossom bud, but which is pushed off as the stamens press harder and harder against it in their effort to greet the happy sunshine. Well, this tiny lid is really the five sepals of the flower joined together. My sepals, however, are not joined all the way up; they are separated from one another at the tips and, while my flowers are still in bud, can be seen folded right over and protecting them. They also are covered with a coat of hairs which are red in colour. This coat, as you can imagine, makes my buds very pretty and cosy-looking. Then, when they unfold into flowers, my bush seems overladen with their wealth of cream-coloured stamens.

I have no petals which could attract insects to my flowers, so those stamens not only have to hold the pollen, but to make themselves attractive as well. They never feel imposed upon, however, as both tasks give them the greatest enjoyment. There are many of them in each flower, and they are arranged around a little cup from the centre of which grows the short pistil. This cup also holds the most delicious honey; so I hardly need tell you that when my bush is in bloom, it is simply crowded with bees, beetles and other insects—all of them having a feast of honey.

Of course, there are many kinds of Native Apple trees, and I am the smallest of them—as you can guess from my name, Dwarf Apple. But

* ANGOPHORA lanceolatus.

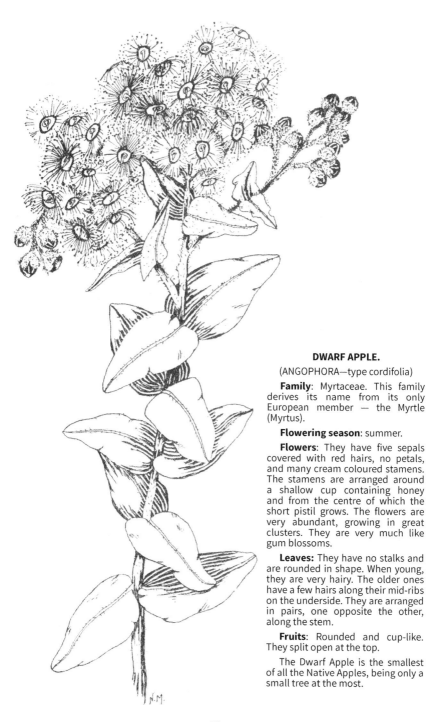

DWARF APPLE.

(ANGOPHORA—type cordifolia)

Family: Myrtaceae. This family derives its name from its only European member — the Myrtle (Myrtus).

Flowering season: summer.

Flowers: They have five sepals covered with red hairs, no petals, and many cream coloured stamens. The stamens are arranged around a shallow cup containing honey and from the centre of which the short pistil grows. The flowers are very abundant, growing in great clusters. They are very much like gum blossoms.

Leaves: They have no stalks and are rounded in shape. When young, they are very hairy. The older ones have a few hairs along their mid-ribs on the underside. They are arranged in pairs, one opposite the other, along the stem.

Fruits: Rounded and cup-like. They split open at the top.

The Dwarf Apple is the smallest of all the Native Apples, being only a small tree at the most.

I have often heard it said that I am the favourite amongst humans because of my very shortness, which makes my large and abundant flowers so easy to reach.

The name by which botanists call me (Angophora) come from two Greek words, one meaning "cup," and the other "carrying"—and refers to my cup-like fruits.

Now, we Native Apples do not grow all over Australia—only in the eastern part of it; and I cannot live comfortably outside New South Wales. But there are so many likenesses between us that you need only be familiar with one of us to be able to recognise the rest of us. I think you know me fairly well now, don't you? You must just remember that all my brothers and sisters are taller than I am, and that some of them have pointy leaves, and you will easily know them wherever you see them.

We are proud of the family likeness we bear to Eucalyptus flowers, for they are such distinguished relations, don't you think?

"'Now what is the flower, the ae first flower
    Springs either on moor or dale;
And what is the bird, the bonnie, bonnie bird,
    Sings on the evening gale?'—

'The primrose is the ae first flower
    Springs either on moor or dale;
And the thistlecock is the bonniest bird
    Sings on the evening gale.'"

—From "Proud Lady Margaret" (an old Scotch ballad)

The Story of the Wild Violet Fairy

(VIOLA—type hederacea)

There was a little creek in Fairyland long, long ago—a little sparkling creek that seemed to be made of all the jewels in the world melted together; and unlike many of its brothers and sisters throughout the world, it flowed along its tiny, narrow path as silently as the moon rises up on the starry sky.

There were no rocks or pebbles in its way to hinder it—nothing whatsoever—and when you looked into it, you could see only reflections. Sometimes, you would wonder what there existed below them, at the very bottom of the creek; and after looking into it as deeply as you could for a long time, you would decide that it was simply reflections all the way down.

Well, we fairies and elves used to love this tiny brooklet very much indeed. We used to sit beside it and tell it all our secrets and ask its advice on many things. But, far from being of a talkative nature, it always remained perfectly silent and was never once known to answer a single question or make the slightest remark.

So we used to flutter about it, and have jumping contests over it until the hills and valleys of Fairyland would resound with our merriment. Then, when we were too tired to play, we would sit down again on its banks, dangling out feet in it and chattering together the whole afternoon.

Of course, when night began to fall, all the fairies would gradually fly away—some to their homes, others to parties, and still others to glow-worm lighted ballrooms.

But mostly, I would stay behind, and very soon I would be left quite alone on the brink of the sparkling water (now even more beautiful than before, because the moon and countless stars were reflected in it.)

There was nothing in the whole of Fairyland that I loved as much as my silent and beautiful friend. And, although it never once spoke to me, I used to feel that it, too, was fond of me; for in winter-time, when all the elves would be shivering with cold, I would go down to the little creek, and when I dangled my feet in it, it would flow over them with tingling warmth. And when it was hot summer-time, it would flow over them with icy cold.

But after many, many years of fairy-happiness had passed by, something sad and terrible happened: humans began to live on Earth, and to growl at and hate each other. They seemed to hate all Nature as well (as far as I

70

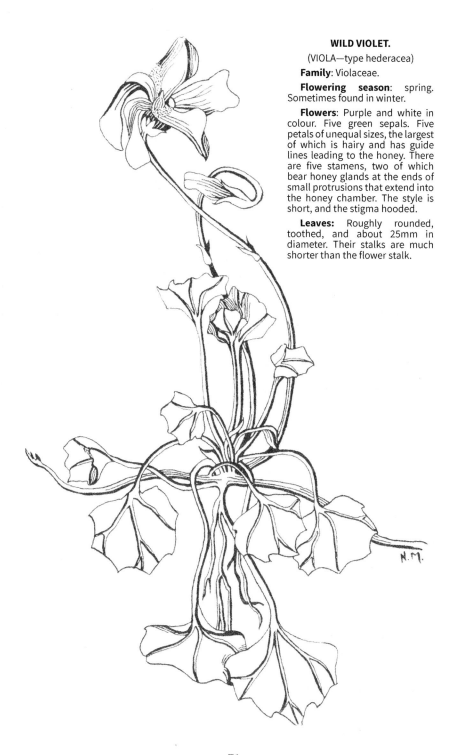

WILD VIOLET.

(VIOLA—type hederacea)

Family: Violaceae.

Flowering season: spring. Sometimes found in winter.

Flowers: Purple and white in colour. Five green sepals. Five petals of unequal sizes, the largest of which is hairy and has guide lines leading to the honey. There are five stamens, two of which bear honey glands at the ends of small protrusions that extend into the honey chamber. The style is short, and the stigma hooded.

Leaves: Roughly rounded, toothed, and about 25mm in diameter. Their stalks are much shorter than the flower stalk.

could see) for they started straight away to cut down our lovely trees, to tread upon our mossy carpets, to root out our ferns and flowers, to break through our very haunts, to tear away our tiny bridges of vines and creepers; for, you see, the Earth that you know now was Fairyland before.

Oh, it was so cruel and horrible that we fairies could live no longer in the world which had been our own for thousands of ages.

There was a wonderful country far beyond the sunset, though, as yet untouched by mortal hands. And that was where we all decided to go, and to make new homes, where none could hurt us.

But it was ever so hard to part with all the magic, secret haunts we had loved. And I felt that I could **never** part with my little voiceless creek. However, the day came at last when I knew I would have to depart; and I went sorrowfully down to the ferny banks to say farewell. But as I leaned down over them to kiss them, two large tears gathered in my eyes and fell into the crystal waters. Then instantly, as if those tears had awakened some long-pondered thought into sound, I heard a murmuring voice coming to me from the very depths of the creek of reflections:

"Violet, little Violet, stay with me. Do not leave me. I would dry away into the earth forever if you say good-bye to me. Turn yourself into a flower bearing the same name as your name and the same colour as your eyes and your pretty frock—and wander along my banks forever!"

And that was exactly how Wild Violets first began to grow, little human, and how they will grow until the end of time, sitting upon the banks of gurgling rivulets and gazing into their depths the whole day long.

"A violet by a mossy stone,
Half hidden from the eye;
    —Fair as a star, when only one
Is shining in the sky."

—Wordsworth.

The Rose Heath Fairy

(BAUERA—type rubioides)

Here, on the mainland of Australia, I am quite a harmless little plant, gently wandering about amongst the ferns that grow deep down in dark green gullies. But in Tasmania, I am not nearly as well behaved, and consequently people do not think very kindly of me; for there, I twine in and out and around things so much—my rambling wiry plant becoming so tangled and interfering so much in the affairs of other plants—that even humans simply cannot make their way through me, and call me a terrible nuisance as well as other things that are not over complimentary.

However, I do not really mind such treatment and so, towards those who are calling me gruff names, I turn my little pale-pink flowers, which always have the art of looking innocent and sweet.

And in this way, I mostly win the good favour of mortals who are kind; although the less gentle ones still continue to grumble and to stamp their feet upon me just as if I had never tried to appeal to them at all. Such is the manner of mortals.

Well, although I am not entirely uncared for, neither am I, as a general rule, cherished amongst the wildflowers of Australia.

When this sorrow becomes more than I can bear, I hold up my pretty rose-like flowers as high as I can and remind people that the beautiful and famous Christmas Bush* belongs to exactly the same family as I do, and therefore can be considered my very near relation. It is only reflected glory on my part, I suppose, but it certainly does win me much respect, and I lift my head up just a wee bit higher on account of it.

A little Rose Heath white or pink,
Who flowers when all the bird-choirs sing,
Who flowers when all the world is young,
Who flowers in summer and in spring.

A Rose Heath bloom, so frail of form,
So delicate and sweet of hue,
That none would think its tangling stems
Could ever vex or worry you!

* CERATOPETALUM gummiferum.

ROSE HEATH.

(BAUERA—type rubioides)

Family: Cunoniaceae.

Flowering season: Spring and summer.

Flowers: Pink in colour. They have four to ten reddish sepals, four to ten large free pink petals, and many stamens.

Leaves: Arranged opposite to one another. They have no stalks. Each consists of three leaflets which are oblong in shape, and toothed. Each leaflet is about 12mm long.

N.M.

The Hyacinth Orchid Fairy

(DIPODIUM—type punctatum)

'Tis true that all the fairies say I am terribly vain and tease me any amount about it. Well, don't you think I have something to be vain about with a delicate summer frock of pink flower-satin, made in dainty flounces, and a dear little petal with a fur coat, and such a majestic height?

Perhaps you are wondering how I happen to possess those tiny dark pink spots all over my petals, are you? It is rather a mischievous story accomplished by an elf who thought I was really far too conceited, so I think you would enjoy it.

A little elf in search of fun
One time, as day had just begun,
Stole forth from Fairyland to where
The giants of Fire had built their lair;
And soon he found his little plot
Was one intolerably hot.
Still, round the flames he wildly flew,
For somewhere there he right well knew
There lived, our sky-roof to adorn
The rosy colour of the morn.
At last a secret nook he eyed,
And peering in it, he espied
A monstrous pot of rich, pink paint;
And as but little of the saint
Within him dwelt, that naughty elf
Gave brush and paint-pot to himself:
He filled an acorn to the brim,
Then, lest the giants should capture him,
Flew quickly down upon the earth,
His little spirits full of mirth;
And fluttered round the woods till he,
In giggling merriment, met me;
And on my face so free from taint,
He sprinkled all his stolen paint.
Then somewhat shy, the guilty elf
To Fairyland betook himself!
And hence those spots of darker pink—
They're rather pretty, don't you think?

HYACINTH ORCHID.
(DIPODIUM—punctatum)

Family: Orchidaceae.

Flowering season: Summer, autumn, and sometimes winter.

Flowers: Usually pink in colour and spotted. The lip is small and furry. There are many flowers on the one stalk, which is brown in colour.

Leaves: Only tiny brown scales at the base of the stem which bears the flowers.

Roots: Thick. Many a plant which steals food from another plant is a "fungus." However, not every fungus is a thief, and it is one of this kinder sort that lives with the roots of the Hyacinth Orchid.

77

The Trigger Plant Fairy
(STYLIDIUM—type graminifolium)

It is more or less unusual to see any sharp, rapid movement in flowers. Of course, what goes on at the magic hour is quite another story; but it is a secret that humans can never know. So it is that in the minds of even the cleverest mortals we, the many inhabitants of Flower Kingdom, are looked upon as unintelligent, thoughtless little beings with life and very little else.

Well, as I come under the laws of the Flower King, I cannot disclose what goes on at the magic hour; but I **can** say this; that there are many, many things which mortals never dream of, and that even "feelingless" objects have souls.

Now, I am one of the few wildflowers that keep a wee bit of their liveliness even during daylight hours. My Orchid friend, Ptetostylis longifolia is another, and as she has been given the same names for the parts of her flower as I have, and as we both do very nearly the same thing, the story she tells will also explain to you a portion of mine. But unlike her, mosquitoes very seldom even come near me, and my "column" instead of my "labellum" is responsible for the "springing."

It is when I receive a visit from the little black bush bee that my column prepares itself for action. And this is just how it happens: Ms. Bee comes flying along looking for honey, and when she sees me, with my four outspread, pink petals, she dives down head first right on top of me.

Now, she always lands exactly opposite my column (which is made up of my stamens and pistils all in one), and once there, she finds that there are tiny spikes on all my petals, which I have put there to guide her in the right direction. This direction is "tight" not only for her (because it leads her to the honey) but also for me (because it enables me to sprinkle her with pollen.)

Well, to continue the story, Ms. Bee goes clumsily forward until she runs, again head first, into my column. When this happens she gets quite a shock, for that mischievous young column quickly springs over on her back and makes her prisoner.

Needless to say, she struggles very hard to free herself, and while she does so I have a wonderful opportunity to dust her all over with pollen.

Then at last she escapes, feeling very hot and very bothered— as you

TRIGGER PLANT.

(STYLIDIUM—type graminifolium)

Family: Stylidiaceae.

Flowering season: Spring, summer, autumn, and sometimes early winter.

Flowers: Pink in colour. There are five petals, the bases of which are united in a short tube. Four of them are large and outspread, each with a small outgrowth which guides the pollinating insect to the honey. The fifth petal ("labellum") is curved back, and is smaller than the other four. It has two outgrowths which guide the column back after it has "sprung". This "springing" is caused by the insect, whose head comes into contact with it. It springs on his back, and as he struggles to escape he becomes sprinkled with pollen.

There are usually many flowers on the tall stem. The sepals (joined to form a tube), the short flower stalks, and the under surface of the four outspread petals are covered with sticky hairs.

Leaves: Grass-like, and growing in a tuft, from the centre of which the stalk bearing all the flowers arises.

79

can well imagine. And while she is flying away as fast as her wings will carry her, I call out to her, in flower-language:

"Good-bye, Ms. Bush Bee, and I hope you enjoyed your honey!"

This makes her even more disgruntled. She mutters a lot of things to herself, and vows she will never go near any flower of my likeness again. But somehow or other she does; and at times she even comes back to me myself, without knowing it. She is a nice little lady, and never one to stay offended very long.

Yes, like my Orchid friend Pterostylis longifolia, I also have a labellum, and although it is not the chief actor in the small drama I have just related, it **has** got its own little part to play; for on its upper edge there are two more tiny spikes, whose duty it is to guide my column back into its position again, after it has finished teasing poor, harmless Ms. Bee.

Of course, when insects are having a day at home and are refusing to visit me, my column has nothing to do, and so remains quite still and sometimes (I fear) goes to sleep. Also, it is inclined to feel a bit sleepy when the day is cool and damp instead of warm and dry.

And now, just one more thing I must tell you, which is to look at my small, stiff sepals, and the underside of my petals, and the short stalks which attach each of my flowers to my main stem (or peduncle). If you look closely enough, you will see that they are covered with the tiniest and stickiest hairs which very soon chase away those naughty insects that have planned to come into my flower through the back door and steal my valuable honey.

Ariel:

> "Where the bee sucks there suck I:
> In a cowslip's bell I lie;
> There I couch when owls do cry.
> On the bat's back I do fly
> After summer merrily.
> Merrily, merrily shall I live now
> Under the blossom that hangs on the bough."
>
> —Shakespeare

The Dandelion Fairy

(TARAXACUM—type densleonis)

Happy little carefree flower
By the roadside growing—
Children love to see my blooms
In the sunshine glowing,
Yet that precious, brilliant gold
(Which all people may behold)
Never, since the world began,
Has been craved by any man!

Fluffy, snowy "puff-o'clocks"
By the roadside growing—
Children love those "parachutes"
In the breezes blowing.
What a happy little band!
Are they bound for Fairyland?
Are they fairies in disguise,
Flying 'gainst the azure skies?

It is in lawns and at the borders of flower-beds (where I know very well I should not be) that I, a member of the famous Daisy family, like best to live. You see, although grown-up humans are hardly ever interested in me, I am interested in them. I do enjoy studying their various gestures and facial expressions. This study is more enlightening than you may imagine, for when the most even-tempered man comes across me in the middle of his favourite flower-bed, I have the pleasure of seeing him in a mood quite different from his usual one.

Little children are different, though, and are always delighted when they find me by the roadside or in meadows. They pick as many of my flowers as their hands will hold, then sit down and make "daisy chains" of them. Perhaps there is nothing I love more than to see children twining me around their heads or shoulders and, thus adorned, skipping merrily home.

The butterflies also are my friends; they flutter around me and lazily take a sip of honey now and then. They are beautiful, idle, posing little creatures, so different from the buzzing, ever active bees that, with a very business-like air, visit one flower after another, then immediately fly away, not wasting a single moment. Beetles also come to me sometimes. They are certainly not as dainty as butterflies or as industrious as bees. What **they** like is a long rambling talk—and once they start, I never can stop them, or get a word of my own in, either, for that matter. Then there are the flies—the

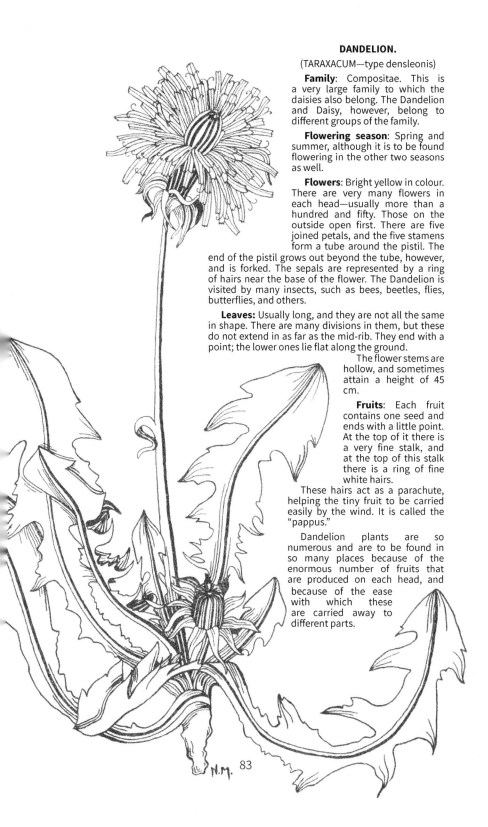

DANDELION.

(TARAXACUM—type densleonis)

Family: Compositae. This is a very large family to which the daisies also belong. The Dandelion and Daisy, however, belong to different groups of the family.

Flowering season: Spring and summer, although it is to be found flowering in the other two seasons as well.

Flowers: Bright yellow in colour. There are very many flowers in each head—usually more than a hundred and fifty. Those on the outside open first. There are five joined petals, and the five stamens form a tube around the pistil. The end of the pistil grows out beyond the tube, however, and is forked. The sepals are represented by a ring of hairs near the base of the flower. The Dandelion is visited by many insects, such as bees, beetles, flies, butterflies, and others.

Leaves: Usually long, and they are not all the same in shape. There are many divisions in them, but these do not extend in as far as the mid-rib. They end with a point; the lower ones lie flat along the ground.

The flower stems are hollow, and sometimes attain a height of 45 cm.

Fruits: Each fruit contains one seed and ends with a little point. At the top of it there is a very fine stalk, and at the top of this stalk there is a ring of fine white hairs.

These hairs act as a parachute, helping the tiny fruit to be carried easily by the wind. It is called the "pappus."

Dandelion plants are so numerous and are to be found in so many places because of the enormous number of fruits that are produced on each head, and because of the ease with which these are carried away to different parts.

N.M. 83

poor despised little flies. They always seem rather fond of me—I suppose because I am a poor, despised little weed.

My native home is not Australia—it is Europe and Asia. But I am able to live in any country at all, as long as it is not too hot in summer or too cold in winter.

Now, some flowers find travelling difficult, and so cannot visit other countries of the world with ease. But in this I am very fortunate, as Nature has provided each of my seeds with a white, fluffy "parachute." It looks frail enough, I know, but it enables my seed to travel for great distances over both land and sea, if necessary. The slightest breeze is sufficiently powerful to carry it away with its precious little cargo. Of course, when the seed finds herself in a piece of ground that she likes, she decides at once to settle down. The wee "parachute" soon falls away from her, so that the wind will not be able to carry her away any more—and before very long, that seed has grown into a new Dandelion plant. That is why the gardener feels so hostile to "puff-o'clocks"; for as he cannot chase and catch every "parachute" he sees, he knows that in a short time he will have to go about pulling out ever so many more Dandelion plants than he had dreamed of. Poor gardener! Although I am loyal to myself (as we all are) I cannot help feeling sorry for him sometimes.

But again I discover that I am not neglected by the goodwill of all humans— even when "parachutes" appear. Perhaps now, more than ever before, children love me. They tell the time by me (as fairies do) and watch the flight of the tiny travellers until, on a windy day, they can be seen no longer.

Of course, you know that each of them is formed from a separate flower; and as every Dandelion "flower" (as you call it) is really composed of over a hundred and fifty tiny yellow blooms, the number of "parachutes" is very great indeed. No wonder the gardener feels worried when he sees them!

What a happy little band!
Are they bound for Fairyland?
Are they fairies in disguise,
Flying 'gainst the azure skies?

"When rosy May comes in wi' flowers,
To deck her gay, green-spreading bowers,
Then busy, busy, are his hours,
    The gardener wi' his paidle."*
The crystal waters gently fa',
The merry birds are lovers a',
The scented breezes round him blaw—
    The gard'ner wi' his paidle."

—Burns

*Hoe.

The Native Fuchsia

(EPACRIS—type longiflora)

Unlike most wildflowers, whose favourite seasons are spring and summer, my favourite of the whole four is winter. Of course, I do stay in Bushland sometimes to see the arrival of beautiful Lady spring. But to see my own little red and white bell-shaped flowers shedding a tiny splash of colour through the forest when it is otherwise sad and cold is really a great enjoyment to me.

Sometimes I visit the open plains, and say, "How do you do?" to the shrubs and grasses. But mostly it is the moist, shady gullies that I haunt, and the rocks around waterfalls. There, my long and somewhat untidy little shrub straggles about aimlessly, and my plentiful flowers hang down gracefully side by side, dreaming and nodding together and sometimes blowing back and forth more violently in the strong, cold wind.

If you were to listen ever so carefully as you were going past me, and if your ears had just a little magic in them, perhaps you would hear me sing:

> Little bells of red and white,
> Swaying on a dainty stem,
> Winter raindrops on us fall—
> It is we who welcome them:
> Other flowers were made so shy
> That they fear a clouded sky.
>
> And, when autumn days have flown
> Where the weary seasons go,
> All the blossoms fade away,
> Saying they refuse to grow
> While the winds are blowing strong
> Past their petals all day long.
>
> But I love to feel my flowers
> Shuffled roughly to and fro.
> It is then that fairy ears,
> List'ning where the wild winds blow,
> From the mossy, ferny dells
> Hear the tinkling of my bells—
> Ringing, ringing day and night,
> Little bells of red and white!

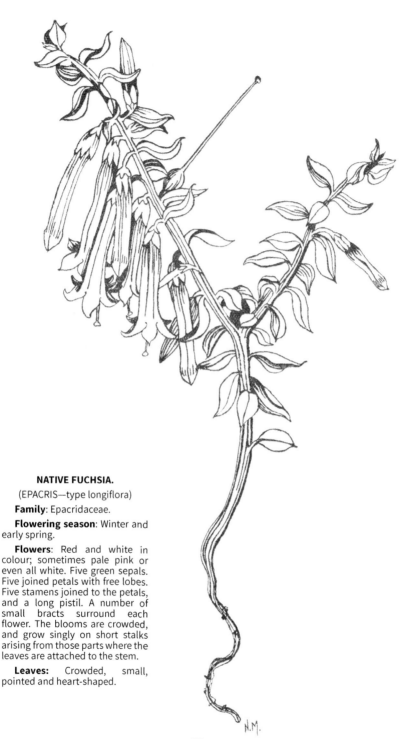

NATIVE FUCHSIA.

(EPACRIS—type longiflora)

Family: Epacridaceae.

Flowering season: Winter and early spring.

Flowers: Red and white in colour; sometimes pale pink or even all white. Five green sepals. Five joined petals with free lobes. Five stamens joined to the petals, and a long pistil. A number of small bracts surround each flower. The blooms are crowded, and grow singly on short stalks arising from those parts where the leaves are attached to the stem.

Leaves: Crowded, small, pointed and heart-shaped.

N.M.

The Burr Buttercup Fairy

(RANUNCULUS—type lappiaceus)

Little golden buttercup nodding to and fro,
Spring and early summer—that is when I grow.
A tiny bag of honey upon each petal lies,
To which come all the busy bees and all the butterflies.
They tell me lovely stories of strange and wondrous things
That in the world are happ'ning. You see, they all have wings—
And while I have to live in soil and dream the hours away,
I always see them soar and whirl and dance the live-long day.
At times I wish that I could change my petals gold for wings;
That I could pass the garden wall and meet those wondrous things.
But no! My fate is not to roam—
The Mother Earth is e'er my home!
For while the world was very young the sun forgot, one day,
That when the twilight came his beams must all be tucked away.
He left **me** out, and all night long I scanned the forest wild
Until the fairies found me—a little sunlight child.
They said that golden beams, once lost, could ne'er espy again
The magic pathway to the sky. They said I'd search in vain.
And that is why, so long ago,
In woodlands I began to grow—
That on those days when dark, grey clouds obscured the sun's
    warm glow,
I might remain, one brilliant light, a-nodding to and fro!

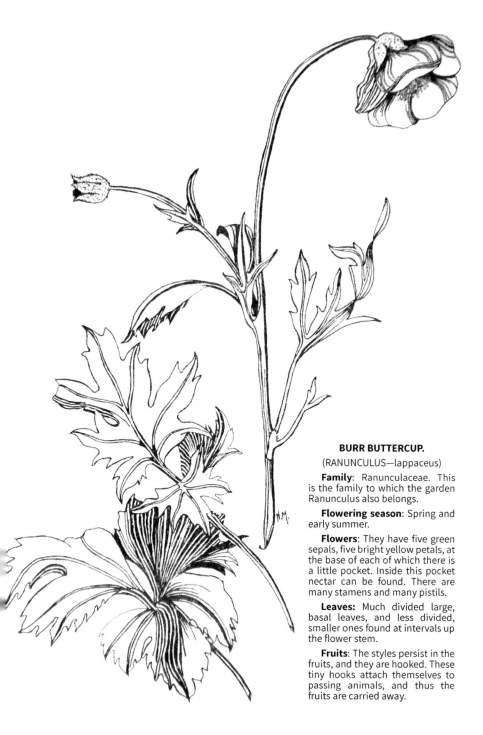

BURR BUTTERCUP.

(RANUNCULUS—lappaceus)

Family: Ranunculaceae. This is the family to which the garden Ranunculus also belongs.

Flowering season: Spring and early summer.

Flowers: They have five green sepals, five bright yellow petals, at the base of each of which there is a little pocket. Inside this pocket nectar can be found. There are many stamens and many pistils.

Leaves: Much divided large, basal leaves, and less divided, smaller ones found at intervals up the flower stem.

Fruits: The styles persist in the fruits, and they are hooked. These tiny hooks attach themselves to passing animals, and thus the fruits are carried away.

The Story of the Christmas Bell Fairy

(BLANDFORDIA—type nobilis)

(Told by MR. HONEYSUCKER)

There is a wonderful spirit of love and kindness which fills the very air at Christmas time, and of which that lovely month of December is formed (I sometimes think). Some people like to call it Santa Claus, others St. Nicholas, others the Three Kings who brought the beautiful gifts to the little child Jesus.

But no matter what one calls it, it still remains; and nearly everyone in the whole wide world feels it. Those who do **not** feel it are unfortunate people indeed.

The fairies, of course, love every name that mortals like to give it. But for themselves, and in Fairyland, it is always known as the Spirit of Giving; for as the end of the year draws near you will notice that everyone wants to give to someone else.

And it is not only humans who feel this Spirit of Giving. It is all the fairies and elves and goblins and gnomes as well. But whereas mortals think only of other mortals, fairies think of the great extensive woodlands—and over them they wave their magic wands of giving.

Then suddenly, the bush awakens into the loveliest blooms, and people, going by, sometimes pick large bunches of them and take them back to their homes in the city, saying:

"Fancy! What glorious Christmas bush!"

And some, whose attention is fastened upon the ground as well as on tall trees, find certain little red and yellow bells, which they also pick and carry home with them. These being another gift of the kind fairies to the Australian bush.

Now, I am really fond of Christmas Bells, that nod together lazily in the summer sunshine, and droop their graceful heads, and whisper secrets to each other which no one ever knows except themselves. I love to flutter all around them and try (without any success) to hear what they are saying. And I love to sip their honey, and feel their soft pollen on my feathers—their pollen which is so delicate that they **must** droop their heads towards the ground in order to protect it from the dampness of the air.

Afterwards, however, when the little case that holds their seeds grows so fast that it is longer than the petals and sepals themselves, then the flowers

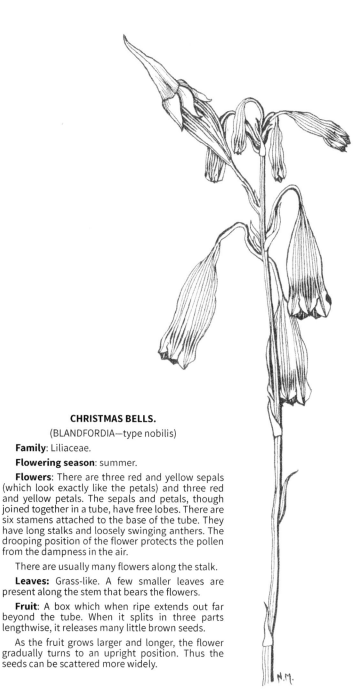

CHRISTMAS BELLS.

(BLANDFORDIA—type nobilis)

Family: Liliaceae.

Flowering season: summer.

Flowers: There are three red and yellow sepals (which look exactly like the petals) and three red and yellow petals. The sepals and petals, though joined together in a tube, have free lobes. There are six stamens attached to the base of the tube. They have long stalks and loosely swinging anthers. The drooping position of the flower protects the pollen from the dampness in the air.

There are usually many flowers along the stalk.

Leaves: Grass-like. A few smaller leaves are present along the stem that bears the flowers.

Fruit: A box which when ripe extends out far beyond the tube. When it splits in three parts lengthwise, it releases many little brown seeds.

As the fruit grows larger and longer, the flower gradually turns to an upright position. Thus the seeds can be scattered more widely.

gradually turn their heads upward,and for the first time they look at the clear, blue sky, and watch the tiny wisps of white clouds drifting across it. That must be indeed a wonderful experience for them.

Of course, when the cases split open and the tiny, rough brown seeds are set free, great Sir Wind takes hold of them and whisks them away in all directions, then drops them down upon the ground and leaves them there to grow into more fine plants with the coming of next summer.

Right through the year I look forward to the coming of the Christmas Bells; and as soon as the very first one has unfolded its red and gold petals, I am there beside it, chattering with it and fluttering all around it (although it is always rather shy, and has very little to say in answer to my numerous questions).

The reason why I am able to pick it out immediately is that my favourite of all colours is red.

> Dainty, dancing Christmas Bells,
> 'Midst the swaying grasses,
> I can see you peeping out
> As the springtime passes—
> Passes from our bushy land
> To some other, distant strand,
> Leaving summer-tide to reign
> O'er the mountain and the plain.
>
> Dainty, dancing Christmas Bells,
> 'Midst the swaying grasses!

The Lord of the Orchid Gnomes

The Orchid Gnome

(CALOCHILUS—type grandiflorus)

Little gnome,
Here I roam
Under bushes evermore
Watching o'er my golden store.

The laws of the bushland and tradition are strange ones, you know. The other day two kookaburras were sitting on a branch of a huge gumtree right beside me. They were holding a sketchy kind of conversation on all manner of trifling things when one, glancing down at me, said to his friend: "Look! There goes the Lord of the Orchid Gnomes—I wonder where he keeps his gold!"

"Well, you'll never find out from him," replied the other. "You know what gnomes are like with their treasure, don't you?"

At this they both broke into peals of laughter, and flew away. But I began to wonder, and I went on wondering: I knew that fairy gnomes had gold, and I knew how carefully they guarded it, mostly around the roots of trees, or in thick, jungly forests—but I was an Orchid gnome, and had no gold at all—at least, not the kind you think of, in big shining nuggets. I have any amount of it in another way; and the funny thing about it is that nearly all plants in the world have it also, yet amongst the fairies, just because I am a gnome, I am the only one to get the credit for it.

Now, can you guess what that gold is? Why, it is the most beautiful of all—it is sunshine. And oh, how eager I am to capture those beams of light! Because, you see, as soon as I do, I have the magic power which only flowers possess of making the sweetest sugar with it, which I store away in my stems for when I may need it.

Perhaps you have never heard before how particular sunbeams are about what kind of thing they are captured by; for they are very lovable, industrious helpers to the earth, and so they refuse to be caught by anything which they feel is not going to use them thoroughly; and as it is only the green parts of any plant that can make sugar out of them, they take in the cooler red and blue colours of the rainbow and entrap them into making sugars out of water and the air around us, while they reflect back to us the hotter green portion which they cannot use so well. Aren't they cunning little things? You know, I wonder if you have ever thought of it, but every single green leaf which you see in your garden is really exactly the same as a little factory. So you just think how many factories you have all around you! And I don't suppose you thought you had one. Well, when my long,

GREAT BEARD ORCHID.

(CALOCHILUS—type grandiflorus)

Family: Orchidaceae.

Flowering seasons: Spring and early summer.

Flowers: Pale green and yellow in colour—sometimes quite a dark green. The labellum is large and covered with long purplish-red hairs. There are several blooms on the one stem.

Leaves: Long and narrow.

The plant is very graceful and sometimes 60cm high.

brown roots drink in little draughts of water from the earth and pass them along my stems until they finally enter my leaves, the tiny machines of all those factories begin to busy themselves, and the magic power which makes them able to work is the warmth of sunbeams.

And, try as people in your mortal world have done, to make sugar by themselves, they have really never succeeded, and always come back to us, asking us how we can possibly do it; but we hold that great secret forever within us. Now, if some cruel giant came along and swept every plant off the earth, what do you think would become of you, with no more bon-bons, or chocolates, or jellies? But, don't let us talk about it, shall we? It would be all too terrible, and there isn't any such giant after all.

And, by the way, I have a long, red beard, which is most attractive, and which I do hope you will take special notice of next time you meet me in the bushlands.

> Gold, gold is the blazing sun,
> For Orchid gnomes to hold—
> Hold, hold in their leaves of green;
> Gold are the sunbeams—gold!

"Each flower the dews have lightly wet,
And in the sky the stars are met,
And on the wave is deeper blue,
And on the leaf a browner hue,
And in the heaven that clear obscure,
So softly dark, and darkly pure,
Which follows the decline of day,
As twilight melts beneath the moon away."

—Byron

The Australian Bluebells
(WAHLENBERGIA—type gracilis)

There is a secret time of night when all the woods are magic—a beautiful time, lit by the twinkling stars, and otherwise wrapped in a cloak of deepest darkness. Mortals call it the "magic hour" and think it is always at midnight. And this is usually true, because, you see, the woods must be entirely free from humans before fairies can appear.

But in those **very** secret haunts, where mortal feet have never yet trodden upon the rich carpets of ferns and mosses, no sooner has the sunset faded and the twilight deepened than all the wildflowers come to life, as it were, and suddenly the bush is filled with tiny, fragile creatures who sail upon the wind and flutter to and fro like butterflies and soar high into the heavens and trip lightly as thistledown over the grass. They dance to the music of the gentle winds and in the soft brilliance of the stars, until a faint colouring in the east proclaims approaching day.

And it is to the chiming of my little bells of blue that the wildflowers listen. It is in answer to their call that they leave their trees or bushes and cast aside their frail disguise, becoming the sweetest and most beautiful of tiny beings that the world has ever seen.

Hush! Hush! For the sun has set,
The sun has set in the flaming west.
Hush! Hush! For the sounds of men
Have crept away to their welcome rest.

Wild winds, cease from your furious play,
And still your wrath for a little space,
For the woods are lonely and gone is the day,
And the nook you see is a fairy place!

Your boist'rous frolic for open hills
And frowning boulders and wastes was made,
But not for the magic of hidden rills
And the witching spell of a fairy glade.

Then come, ye fairies! I call you! List
To the tinkling sound of my bells of blue!
Oh, come, by the stars and moonbeams kissed,
To dance on the billows of falling dew!

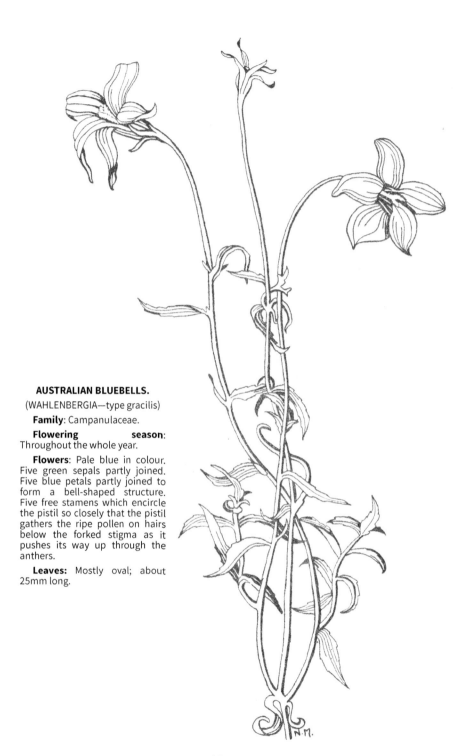

AUSTRALIAN BLUEBELLS.

(WAHLENBERGIA—type gracilis)

Family: Campanulaceae.

Flowering season:
Throughout the whole year.

Flowers: Pale blue in colour. Five green sepals partly joined. Five blue petals partly joined to form a bell-shaped structure. Five free stamens which encircle the pistil so closely that the pistil gathers the ripe pollen on hairs below the forked stigma as it pushes its way up through the anthers.

Leaves: Mostly oval; about 25mm long.

99

The Lillipilly Fairy

(EUGENIA—type Smithii)

In spring and summertime the fairies are very happy, for in these seasons many more wildflowers come out than in any other —and fairies do love wildflowers.

Now I, the Lillipilly, also come out in tiny white blooms at these times, and you should just see the elves standing beside me clapping their hands with joy because they know that very soon my tree will be covered with big, round balls for them to play with.

My flowers grow together in large groups near the ends of branches; and it is a good thing they do, for if they did not, I am afraid no-one would notice them (as they are by no means big and handsome). Then, when the tiny sepals and petals and frail stamens shrivel away, the little balls begin to grow. Each one has a thin stem and when, after a short time, it decides to grow no more, it looks just like a beautiful cherry; but instead of being dark red in colour, it is pink and cream.

You can imagine, I am sure, how pretty my tree looks when it is covered with heavy bunches of purple, pink and cream balls, nestling in amongst the large, dark green leaves. Human children always seem to be ever so excited when they find me, at the side of a river or deep down in shady gullies. But the only thing they are sorry about is that almost as soon as they pick a branch of me laden with berries, the pretty balls begin to fall off one after the other until there are very few left.

"Oh," they sigh in disappointment, "the fairies did use bad gum when they were sticking these lillipillies on!" But they little know that the fairies are hovering all around them and can hear everything they say. Those tiny mischievous creatures with their gossamer frocks and sunshine wings laugh merrily to themselves, for it is they who, all unknown, are knocking off the berries as quickly as they can—because they know quite well that children have their own toys to play with and do not need the pretty soft, pink lillipillies with which the fairies love to play ball at the magic hour.

Oh, hide them, hide them behind those rocks,
Oh, pop them quickly in a deep, dark box—
Oh, hold them tightly and fly as fast
As elves and goblins when the night has passed!

And if you hide them where none can see,
And if you even as the lightning flee,
You'll still discover the elves have found
And knocked your berries to the soft, warm ground!

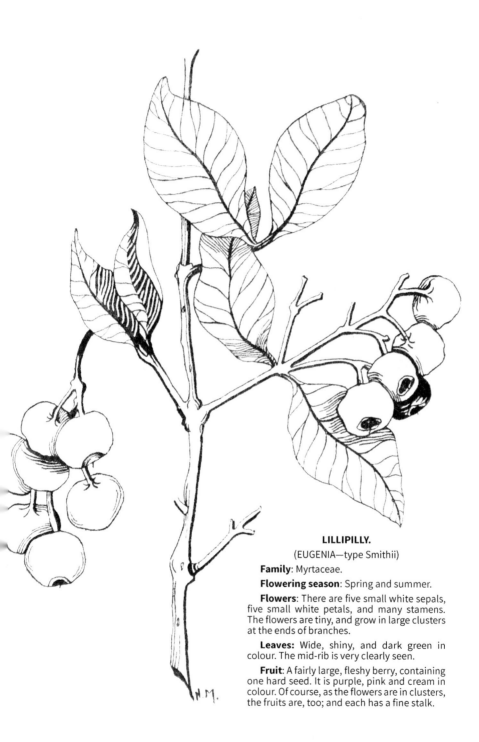

LILLIPILLY.

(EUGENIA—type Smithii)

Family: Myrtaceae.

Flowering season: Spring and summer.

Flowers: There are five small white sepals, five small white petals, and many stamens. The flowers are tiny, and grow in large clusters at the ends of branches.

Leaves: Wide, shiny, and dark green in colour. The mid-rib is very clearly seen.

Fruit: A fairly large, fleshy berry, containing one hard seed. It is purple, pink and cream in colour. Of course, as the flowers are in clusters, the fruits are, too; and each has a fine stalk.

The Growl of the Orchid Scrooge

(LYPERANTHUS—type nigricans)

Happy little child, pass by me,
And the songs of bell-birds follow;
Seldom do my flowers adorn me,
For my heart is full of sorrow.

And you will not find me dancing with the sunshine and shadows as do other wildflowers, for I much prefer sad loneliness; so I hardly ever come out in flowers at all, because I know that if I should, other fairies and elves, birds, mosquitoes and beetles would come and talk to me, bothering me with ceaseless conversation and playful tricks. All this nonsense I **cannot** bear, so, as I must put in some appearance upon the earth, I send up above the ground a funny, thick dwarf of a plant with a large, oval-shaped leaf—none of these flimsy-looking things; and I give it a respectable colour of as dark a green as Nature can possibly find for me.

In the meantime I stay well and truly underneath, where I cannot hear such exasperating gossip as, for instance:

"—Did you hear about Billie the bee yesterday, drinking so much honey out of Miss Waratah's honeypot that she was too drunk to see straight, and had to stumble upon a moss-bed near the Diamond Creek and stay there for over two hours?" or "— Did you know that Miss Isabelle Butterfly stayed out so late last night inquiring into the details of Mrs. Dragonfly's trip abroad to the other side of Crystal Lake that she couldn't find her way home and has been missing ever since?"

You can surely see how tired I must get with all this—what shall I call it? Underneath the ground is much quieter: I can sit there for months at a time, moping, without anyone interfering.

Sometimes, however, I do feel as if I would like to look at the day, so that makes me more miserable, as I cannot see day without coming into contact with the altogether rude and inconsiderate traffic of flying things. But if a bushfire has just passed over the place, leaving it black and lifeless, I smile to myself and pop my head out for a spell of a month or two. And then, if I don't get butterflies and birds and elves, I get humans—and they're worse. They talk and talk, and just because my flowers happen to be rather lovely to look at, with their dark red and purple tones and a little white, they have to pick me and fuss about with me and commit the atrocity of pressing me flat in a book. Of course, when this occurs I think it is time for a little interference on my part; so I turn coal-black all over—that teaches them not to meddle with me! I wonder if this is the only reason mortals have for calling me the "Undertaker."

Well, I am going now—good-bye!

RED BEAKS.

(LYPERANTHUS—type nigricans)

Family: Orchidaceae.

Flowering season: spring.

Flowers: Dark reddish-purple in colour. The sepals and petals are long and narrow. The "tongue" is white, with red veinings on the side-lobes. There are several flowers on the one stalk, but usually they do not appear unless a bushfire has swept over the place where the plants are growing. When dried, the flowers turn black.

Leaves: Large, oval in shape, and mottled.

The whole plant is usually only about 15cm high.

103

The Christmas Bush Fairy

(CERATOPETALUM—type gummiferum)

I suppose you have often heard it said that all nature is in harmony and Man alone is discord. Well, this is not entirely true, for there are wild animals in jungles that fight savagely, whilst in the plant kingdom there is a constant warfare which often results in the destruction or stunting of the smaller by the larger plants.

But I think it is true that men are the greatest destroyers of all, for no sooner have they made their appearance in some beautiful wooded country than the moss is trampled on, the ferns are trodden down and broken, the trees (before so grand and majestic) lie sadly on the ground; then after a time they are set upright once more, with all their leaves and branches broken away, as ugly telegraph poles. You see, we plants are so thoroughly defenceless when humans attack us.

Once upon a time, I thought I was safe, and that no-one would bother cutting me down—because I loved to imagine that I would be of no use to man. But very soon, I found that I had been mistaken; for I was by no means spared the sorrows of my companions. Mortals did not take long to discover that my reddish-coloured, soft wood could be made into tool handles, and many other things. So it was that we handsome trees began to fall, one after another, and at the present time you will seldom find us ten or twelve meters high—except in parts where humans have not bothered us. Mostly you see us only as very young bushes of an unambitious height. You will agree, I think, that such treatment is terribly discouraging.

So often have I heard people remark on my red "petals," that I think I had better make sure you never speak of them in that way, by telling you that they are not petals, but sepals. When my flowers first unfold they are tiny, white, and if it were not for the fact that many of them grow together, they would be hardly noticeable. The sepals are very small indeed, and the petals only a little larger. But as the fruits ripen, these sepals enlarge more and more until they are about 12mm long. At the same time, they change their colour, gradually becoming the loveliest red; and just about Christmas their colour is brightest. It is for this reason that I am called the Christmas Bush.

This is the height of my glory. All the year round I look forward to December, for I do enjoy looking beautiful and decorative—all plants do. Their flowers are their greatest pride.

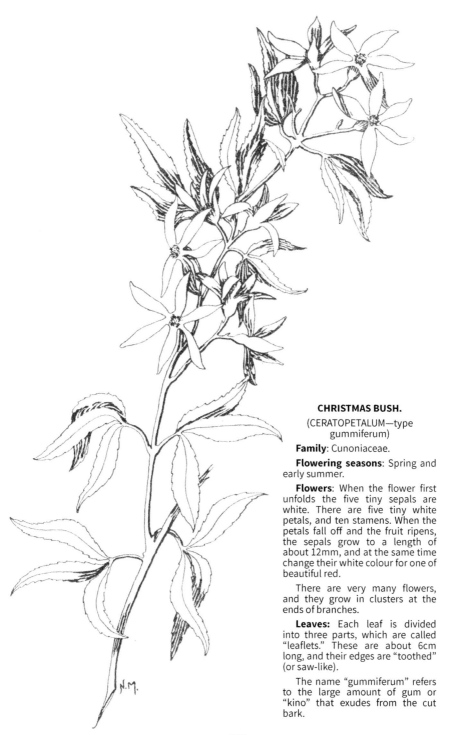

CHRISTMAS BUSH.

(CERATOPETALUM—type gummiferum)

Family: Cunoniaceae.

Flowering seasons: Spring and early summer.

Flowers: When the flower first unfolds the five tiny sepals are white. There are five tiny white petals, and ten stamens. When the petals fall off and the fruit ripens, the sepals grow to a length of about 12mm, and at the same time change their white colour for one of beautiful red.

There are very many flowers, and they grow in clusters at the ends of branches.

Leaves: Each leaf is divided into three parts, which are called "leaflets." These are about 6cm long, and their edges are "toothed" (or saw-like).

The name "gummiferum" refers to the large amount of gum or "kino" that exudes from the cut bark.

Yet alas! Mortals cannot leave me alone even then, but must pick great armfuls of me to ornament their homes, leaving behind them in the bush only a few poor, forlorn little trees robbed of all their beauty.

I suppose I should be less selfish and not mind—but mortals also should be less selfish and not pick, don't you think?

Something else you may not know about me is that right inside my trunk there is a substance that looks like a gum from the plant's sap, but which is really what humans call a "kino" which is a dark red liquid formed mainly in between the bark and the central trunk. This is very pretty indeed, being red and transparent. Kino comes out when the bark is damaged and dries into a shiny, hard, red, and protective solid when the bark is damaged. Kino with its high tannin content is sometimes used as a medicinal treatment.

> Other blossoms lose their charm
> When their petals droop and die.
> Life for them is e'en as short
> As a zephyr's gentle sigh.
> Just a fleeting day or so
> Robs them of their vivid glow.
>
> Yet when all my petals fall,
> Beauty does not sadly fade.
> She, the sweetest fairy-soul—
> Sweetest soul that e'er was made—
> Turns my tree, with magic hand,
> To a crimson Fairyland.

"Thanks to the human heart by which we live,
Thanks to its tenderness, its joys, and fears,
To me the meanest flower that blows can give
Thoughts that do often lie too deep for tears."

—Wordsworth

Another Greenhood Fairy

(PTEROSTYLIS—type pedunculata)

Have you ever heard people say that you have to "train your eye" to the finding of certain things, like four-leafed clovers? Well, a short time ago, two humans were walking together along a bush-track at the side of which I was growing, when one, happening to notice me, said: "Look, there are some little Greenhoods! And there are two kinds of them also." Her friend, of course, looked where she had pointed and after a long while admitted that all she could see was a bit of fallen wood and much grass.

At this, the first speaker laughed heartily, and replied: "Well, they **are** there just the same. And before we return home tonight, you will be able to pick out Greenhoods as quickly as I can, because your eyes will have become accustomed to finding them." This sounded rather strange to me, but that night at the magic hour, I learned from my relations farther along the track that after a very little while, the second speaker did begin to find Greenhoods, and that she couldn't believe they had been as plentiful in the place where I was growing.

"And so," thought I to myself, "I and my fellow Greenhoods must be like four-leafed clovers in at least one respect."

Of course, I can understand why we are somewhat difficult to find. I suppose anything would be, which, growing amongst grasses, was itself green and brownish in colour.

Now, that first speaker whom I told you about must have been a quick observer indeed; for, if you remember, she noticed instantly not only that there were Greenhoods beside her, but also that there were two kinds. And if you look with sufficient care, little human, you will nearly always find that where I grow, that other kind grows, too. And if you happen to notice that other kind first, you are almost sure to meet me also very nearby. Because, you see, Pterostylis nutans and I are very fond of each other, and so we do not like to become separated any more than we possibly can. We are just sufficiently similar to form a link of likeness between us, and just sufficiently different to make us interesting to one another.

Firstly, we both have a spreading rosette of leaves at the base of our plant, and we are both fairly tall; and secondly, while Pterostylis nutans droops her head decidedly, I hold mine perfectly erect. This may not seem very important to humans, but it means a great deal to flowers. For, you understand, I can tell her all that is going on in the sky and when a storm is approaching, and she can tell me all that is going on along the ground and when an ant is approaching.

So that together, we gain quite an all-round knowledge of current events.

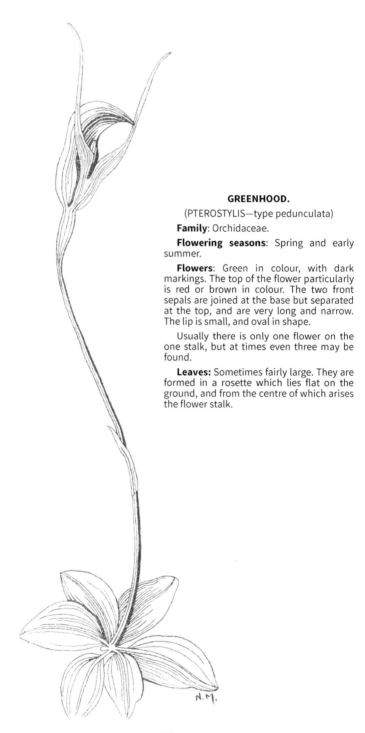

GREENHOOD.

(PTEROSTYLIS—type pedunculata)

Family: Orchidaceae.

Flowering seasons: Spring and early summer.

Flowers: Green in colour, with dark markings. The top of the flower particularly is red or brown in colour. The two front sepals are joined at the base but separated at the top, and are very long and narrow. The lip is small, and oval in shape.

Usually there is only one flower on the one stalk, but at times even three may be found.

Leaves: Sometimes fairly large. They are formed in a rosette which lies flat on the ground, and from the centre of which arises the flower stalk.

The Needle Bush Fairy

(HAKEA—type acicularis)

Of course, I know why it is mortals call me the Needle Bush. It is because of my seemingly vicious leaves—long, narrow, and ending with a sharp point. They are just like rose thorns to **feel**, but to look at they are longer, finer and ever so much more numerous. Also, they are attached all over my stems, so that they stand out in every imaginable direction, and it is not possible for anyone to pick a tiny branch of me without getting badly pricked.

However, every part of me is not cruel, for in early springtime there are to be found amongst my unfriendly leaves the prettiest and gentlest little white or creamish flowers. While they are still in bud, they seem to be only a few stray, curly threads which have caught on to the branch by mistake. But as they unfold, you see that each "thread" is a separate flower, that there are quite a number of these blooms in each group, and that there are many groups all the way up the stem.

These flowers are very kind and mean no harm to anyone. But in reality my leaves are also kind—and I am sure you would agree with me if you knew them properly. You see, because my flowers are so frail and defenceless, they might easily come to much harm at the hands of rough bush creatures and mortals. But as it is, they live quite safely and happily because they know that while my leaves are around them, nothing can hurt them. So, every time you want to say how cruel those "needles" are, you must remember that they are only doing their very best to protect the little flowers you love so much to see. Also, you may notice that although they are more closely crowded together than mortals find convenient, they are quite far enough apart to allow the entrance of gentle insects (such as bees) who come to sip honey, have a little gossip and then carry away some pollen to another Needle Bush flower.

I wonder now if I have made you feel a wee bit more kindly towards my prickly leaves.

I do not for a moment doubt that you are already acquainted with my fruits, which have the queerest bumpy appearance, and end with a funny little point. They are thick and woody. Inside them there are two seeds, each with a pretty wing almost papery to feel. The wing, of course, makes it easy for the seed to fly about in the wind, and not reach the ground too soon, before it has had time to enjoy a few adventures and the fresh, open air.

You will look for me next time you come to the bush, won't you? And I do hope you will make friends with my leaves. They are really lonely little beings because no one ever seems to like them, so they will appreciate your thoughtfulness very much.

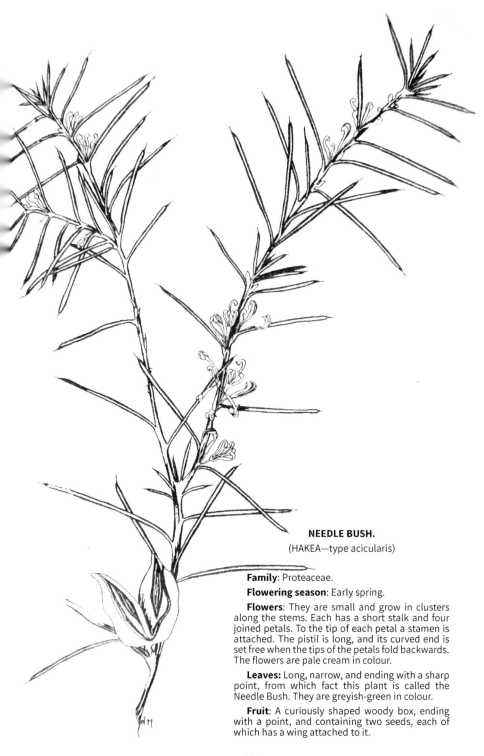

NEEDLE BUSH.

(HAKEA—type acicularis)

Family: Proteaceae.

Flowering season: Early spring.

Flowers: They are small and grow in clusters along the stems. Each has a short stalk and four joined petals. To the tip of each petal a stamen is attached. The pistil is long, and its curved end is set free when the tips of the petals fold backwards. The flowers are pale cream in colour.

Leaves: Long, narrow, and ending with a sharp point, from which fact this plant is called the Needle Bush. They are greyish-green in colour.

Fruit: A curiously shaped woody box, ending with a point, and containing two seeds, each of which has a wing attached to it.

The Rock Lily or Orchid King

(DENDROBIUM—type speciosum)

Do you know when the little silver moonbeams dance from the very top of the sky, along the milky way, through the still, silent trees to the ground, and there play with tiny dewdrops and fluffy-winged moths? Well, it is only at these times that I can easily become a fairy, for I love the moon as other Orchids do the sun, and others, the wind. Of course, I could not live without the good old sun to give me strength and warmth—yet, well, I don't know how it is, but I often think that millions of years ago my frail petals were woven with threads of moonlight as they wandered to the Earth.

I can remember a long time back when all the bush orchids gathered together in a great assembly and, with one voice, proclaimed me their king; and what do you think? So that even humans would realise my all-powerful position they gave my most important petal any amount of purple spots, as we had heard that such a colour to humans was a sign of royalty. And to this very day I still wear them because I think they look so becoming on their creamy background.

And now I must tell you something rather funny which amused me quite a lot. One afternoon in the middle of last September I was giving a garden party to a few of my subjects, amongst whom were little Miss Pink Fingers, or in other words, Lady Caladenia carnea, Lord Calochilus grandiflorus, Countess Dipodium punctatum, and Sir Cryptostylis subulata or, the Knight of the Fairy Garter, as he is usually known.

Just as we were about to ask the earth for a little more water to drink, we heard human voices approaching, so we kept as still and quiet as could be, because we hoped no one would notice us, as mortals always seem to want to pick us and then drop us by the wayside without any thought at all.

Soon, however, a little girl with long, fair hair came running down the bush track, and, her searching eyes having picked us out immediately, she called:

"Oh, Mother, just look at these pretty flowers!" Then she came right up to me and, taking hold of my big, thick stem, she said:

"And look, Mother, here is a Rock Lily!"

We all felt like shrieking with laughter, but of course that would have been terrible.

"Well, don't pick it, dear," said a kind-faced lady, just now making her appearance, "You know, that is one of the protected flowers; and don't pick any of the others, either, for they are all Orchids and also protected."

With this the little girl let me go, and saying: "But aren't they pretty,

ROCK LILY or the ORCHID KING.

(DENDROBIUM—type speciosum)

Family: Orchidaceae.

Flowering season: spring.

Flowers: Creamish-coloured. The lip ("labellum") is beautified with purple spots. Usually the flowers are much crowded together, very numerous and fragrant.

Leaves: Shiny, stiff and leathery. Their mid-rib is very clearly seen.

Stems: Thick, and deeply grooved. It is in the stems that a great deal of the plant's food is stored.

The plant does not grow in the soil, mostly. It is found growing to perfection on trees and rocks. However it does not steal any food from the trees upon which it rests; therefore it is not a parasite.

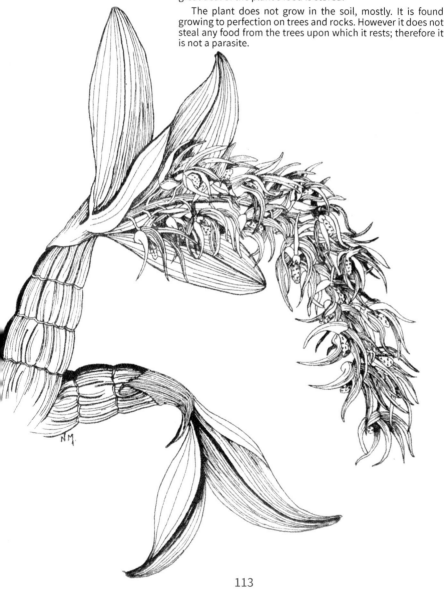

113

Mother, all those pink and white and red and yellow flowers?" she continued her journey along the track.

As soon as they had gone there was a great deal of tittering and giggling and whispering amongst my guests. Little Miss Pink Fingers leaned over to the Knight of the Fairy Garter and whispered something in his ear, to which they both screwed up their eyes and giggled. Lord Calochilus took the Countess's arm and spoke rather seriously, then turning to me, said: "Most mighty sovereign, is it any wonder that humans call you a 'lily,' and a 'rock' one at that, when you keep your stem so ungainly and thick and hard? Is it any wonder that they will not even give you the credit of being an Orchid? Look, for an instance, at the slender daintiness of Miss Pink Fingers, and my friend the Countess!"

At this, both the pretty ladies looked clown to the very tips of their toes and blushed a little pinker than usual.

By this time I thought it would befit me to say something for myself, so I spread out a sheaf of creamy blossoms and said:

"Ah! you little seem to realise that I am your king, and that as such, my position is not a dainty one, but a serious and responsible one: I have to teach you an admiration of determination. It is for this reason that I live on hard, dry rocks, on the faces of cliffs and on the bark of trees—yet I wouldn't think of being a parasite and stealing from them who have such a lot to do to nourish their own tremendous heights and widths."

And so I went on explaining to my now very serious listeners how, because I became hungry the same as they did and needed food, my stems, leaves and roots had to get busy and do all they could to help me. "It is when the rain falls," I continued, "that my opportunity comes. Then my stems, leaves and roots absorb just as many of the raindrops as they can, and store them away in hundreds of little compartments so that in times of drought I shall have plenty of nourishment to go on with. And you well know, because you have them too, those tiny compartments in our stems where we keep the sweetest and finest sugar, which mortals cannot even see without using strong 'glass eyes' as well as their own.

My gallant Knight now stepped forward and knelt before me saying, "Indeed we have a wonderful king in Orchid land, and we are all very proud of you: apart from your beautiful ideals you also have flowers whose whose delicate colour and perfume are admired by every one of your little subjects!"

So that is the story of my garden party in the middle of last September, and of how I let my Orchid guests into a few of my guarded secrets.

I was giving a garden party.

The Tea-tree Fairy

(LEPTOSPERMUM—type flavescens)

Amongst mortals, it is the custom, I have heard, for people to become friends and to seek each other's company when there is a bond of sympathy or affection between them. In the bush world, this is also the case sometimes; although it usually happens that different birds and insects become most friendly with the flowers from which they can easiest sip honey. So it is that Ms. Bee shuns long, narrow, tube-like flowers because these mostly store their honey at the very bottom of their tube, and her tongue is not nearly long enough to reach it. Mr. Honeysucker, on the other hand, is on the best of terms with such flowers, because his beak is long enough.

I wonder if humans always make friends the way I have been told they do, or if they also are over-interested sometimes in how much honey they can get from their fellow humans.

Well, if you look carefully at my cream-coloured flowers, you will see that the five outspread petals are arranged round a sort of shallow little cup which holds the honey. This is **so** shallow, and the sweet liquid it contains is so easily found, that you will at once guess what insect it is who is my special friend—Ms. Bee.

She is the principal one; but, of course, there are many others. In fact, any insect at all with a short tongue and a fondness for honey is likely to visit me quite often. So I am never lonely.

And now, if you look again at the floor of my cup, you will notice that it is divided into five parts; and that as the petals and stamens around it fall away, it becomes the top of my fruit. This fruit enlarges, growing harder and more woody all the time, until finally (when the narrow seeds inside it are ripe, and when the season is dry) it splits open along the now five deep grooves, and the seeds are set free.

I am sure you will not have difficulty in finding me, as I grow in all the eastern parts of Australia. I am a tall shrub and have rather small, oblong leaves which, though green, have a lot of yellow in them too. And of course, you will easily be able to recognise my cream-coloured flowers.

TEA-TREE.

(LEPTOSPERMUM—type
flavescens)

Family: Myrtaceae.

Flowering seasons: Spring
and summer.

Flowers: They have five green
sepals, the bases of which are
joined to form a round tube.
The five petals are outspread
and cream-coloured. There are
many stamens arranged around
a shallow cup, from the centre of
which a short pistil grows, and
which contains honey. The flowers
do not grow in clusters, but singly.

Leaves: About 25mm long,
oblong in shape, and yellowish-
green in colour. They grow fairly
close together.

Fruit: Cup-shaped. When the
seeds are ripe and the season is
dry, the fruit splits open across the
top in five places, and many small
seeds fall out.

The plant is a tall shrub.

117

The Romance of the Little White Dove

(CALADENIA—type praecox)

Have you ever wished from the very bottom of your heart to see a fairy? Have you ever crept on tip-toe from the softly curling fronds of your fernery to a large chrysanthemum or a shy blue violet, and peered right in to see if you could catch one by surprise, and not finding one at all, ask a little tearfully: "Oh, dear Miss Violet, haven't you seen a fairy pass this way to-day?" And that timid flower which was, perhaps, a fairy just pretending all the time, winked at you—and a tiny spark of mischief flashed into the heart of the flower.

Well, while you look so unsuccessfully for fairies, maybe you have heard birds singing way up in the trees. They are really laughing at you, because they can see them everywhere: perched on your hand, ruffling up your hair—you thought it was a breeze that **blew** your hair didn't you? No! It was about half a dozen elves **swinging** on it!

Birds can see and hear fairies easier than any other material creature. And for this reason it was that ever so many years ago, when the world was young and beautiful, I, a little white dove, with a pale pink colour under my wings, used to carry messages from flowers to fairies and from fairies to flowers. I always remember a tiny Microtis Orchid once conveying a message by me to Fairyland: "Please send a squadron of goblins to Grassland Grove—a snail is approaching." Another time, a little spring fairy whispered in my ear: "Hurry down to where the Orchid gnomes are growing, and tell their leader to get all his followers out in flowers during today. At midnight I shall visit them and paint their long beards a brilliant red. They will like that news." Always in these rapid flights of mine I used to think what lovely little beings bushland Orchids were, and right inside me I wished that I could be one too; but I never said a word about it in Fairyland.

One time, though, I was wandering around the bush, talking to this Orchid and that one, and wishing more than ever that I could be one of them when all of a sudden I heard a tiny, very frightened, silvery cry. I flew to where it came from and alas! There, terribly caught and entangled in a great spider web, was the beautiful fairy queen. It was all the work of the Giant of Spiders before he was defeated by the Knight of the Fairy Garter.

I said a few words of comfort and promise to her and then, as fast as my wings could carry me, I flew to where the grand army of dwarfs and goblins was resting, waiting to be called upon, and told them what had happened.

WHITE DOVES.

(CALADENIA—type praecox)

Family: Orchidaceae.

Flowering season: Winter and early spring.

Flowers: White in colour, with pink or green markings. The "tongue" is fringed, and is marked with purple in the centre. Usually there are two or three flowers on the one stem.

This Orchid is to be found only in Victoria, and seldom grows taller than 15 cm.

In less than two seconds the whole army had landed at the entrance to the spider web, and charged right into it. This occupied the Giant while the fairy king unbound his lovely queen, and together they all flew back to Fairyland. Later I heard that the Giant spent two whole days rebuilding his web, it was so huge and strong.

But can you guess what happened? The next evening, when the stars were trooping up in hundreds and thousands to their positions in the sky, the queen sent for me to go to her court, and when I arrived she said that because I had saved her life she would grant me anything my heart desired. I thanked her ever and ever so much, and of course, told her that more than anything in the world I would like to be a little wild Orchid. She smiled, and kissed my head so gently that I shall never forget my joy that night, or her loveliness.

According to her order I was escorted to the mortal world by a whole troop of fairies, as well as by the king and queen themselves. And after much celebration, dancing, singing and laughter, the queen touched me softly with the tip of her wand; and, looking at myself in a tiny brook nearby, I saw the loveliest white flower just streaked with the tiniest bit of pale pink. But the magic wand had touched me so lightly that some of the downy feathers on my head had not quite disappeared, and to this very day they still remain to adorn my smallest petal!

"In all places, then, and in all seasons,
    Flowers expand their light and soul-like wings,
Teaching us, by most persuasive reasons,
    How akin they are to human things."

—Longfellow

The Bottlebrush Fairy

(CALLISTEMON—type lanceolatus)

My name Callistemon comes from two Greek words, one meaning "beauty," the other "stamen." So that the whole name means "beautiful stamen"; and if you remember having seen me in any of your bushwalks, you will realise how it is people call me that.

The anthers of my stamens are rather small and yellow, but the long, fine stalks (or "filaments") are bright red in colour. Each flower has a great many stamens, and as there are any amount of flowers crowded closely together near the tip of the stem, you can understand how pretty and attractive I seem to those who meet me.

I am glad my stamens are so numerous and beautiful, because the rest of my flower is such that no one would ever bother to look at it more than once. My fate would indeed be a sad one if I did not possess those stamens. Why! Not even the Honeysuckers would go to the trouble of visiting and talking to me and, of course, carrying away my pollen to another Bottlebrush somewhere else in Bushland. My five little petals are a brown-yellowy-green colour, and my five sepals are small and green.

Usually, we red Bottlebrush shrubs do not grow separately (that would be lonesome indeed) but many of us together. So that in spring and summer, when we come out in flower, we certainly do add a bright splash of colour to our surroundings. I remember once how a little girl, walking through the bush with her mother and father, came across us and, clasping her hands in admiration, said: "Mother dear, see how the woodlands are blushing!"

If you look at my smooth, oblong leaves, you will see all over them tiny round dots. These, as my friend Boronia has explained to you, are glands filled with oil. However, although we are similar in this, I do not belong to her family, but to that which humans call Myrtaceae. I am proud of this fact, because Myrtaceae is a most distinguished family, having as some of its members the Eucalyptus, the Lillipilly and Teatrees. If your very near relation were a Gum tree or a Lillipilly, wouldn't you feel ever so proud too?

I suppose you have all noticed my little fruits, have you? Of course, as my flowers are crowded together, my fruits are too; and they just look like a whole family of fairy-cups. Now, when the right season comes (that is, when the weather is nice and dry) they all split open at the top and a host of tiny seeds falls out. These are blown away by the wind to their new

BOTTLEBRUSH.

(CALLISTEMON—type
lanceolatus)

Family: Myrtaceae.

Flowering seasons: Spring and summer.

Flowers: There are five small green sepals and five red or dirty green petals. The stamens are very numerous, long, and crimson in colour. Their anthers are yellow. The pistil is also crimson and long.

The flowers are crowded together very closely around the stem, and have no stalks. As red is the favourite colour of Honeysuckers, it is likely that these birds visit the flowers often.

Leaves: They are oblong, and usually about five centimeters long. All over them, tiny oil dots can be seen.

Fruits: Round and woody. They only split open in dry weather, when they release many small seeds.

123

homes—sometimes far away from and sometimes near to the plant from which they came. This is a great adventure for the little seeds, and I can assure you they look forward to it ever so much.

Now, before I say good-bye, I must point out to you something which occurs with all Bottlebrushes. You would think it strange if the stems of roses continued to grow through the tops of the blooms, wouldn't you? And yet, when you see a crowded group of Bottlebrush flowers, you are almost sure to notice growing on above it a leafy shoot, which is really the continuation of the stem. So it is that on a single branch you will often find, first a collection of little fruits; then, above these, a group of flowers; and above these again, the youngest part of the stem growing on and on, which will soon be adorned with another collection of flowers.

This is funny, don't you think? But Bottlebrushes are not the only plants that do it. Next time you go for a bush walk, you could enjoy yourself very much searching for more. And if you were to look at Teatrees (Leptospermums) very carefully, I am sure you would not be disappointed.

Oh the whip-bird's call and the bracken sea,
The green, immortal minstrelsy,
    The tow'ring trees, the mystic glen
    So far from the abodes of men—
A sky-roofed sanctuary of moss and ferns,
Where man the harmonies of Nature learns.

What though a thousand duties to me float
As blatant voices on a city-note?
    Their cruel enslavement I must fly,
    Or in their strangling meshes die!
Here are the curling fronds, the fragrant earth, the flowers,
What else does man require to fill his fleeting hours?

The Heath-Leaved Banksia Fairy

(BANKSIA—type ericifolia)

When I look at the Boronias, Wattles, Teatrees, Flannel Flowers and many others of my bush companions, I begin to realise that there is nothing frail or dainty about me at all. Of course, if it happened that every one of us was dainty, there would be little variation indeed, and humans would soon complain about the monotony of Bushland. So I suppose I should be grateful that at least I can help to make things interesting.

But, despite the thick appearance of my large groups of flowers, I have never heard anyone condemn me as being ugly. On the contrary, everyone seems to praise me for my handsomeness and my flame-like colouring. Sometimes I am only deep yellow, but other times I have, mixed with the yellow, such a brilliant reddish colour, that children imagine me to be a scrap of bushfire captured magic and fastened to my tall, woody shrub.

I wonder if you have ever taken one of those thick, uptight stalks of mine covered with blooms, and counted the number of flowers on it. If you have, no doubt you have been surprised to find that there are several hundreds— each separate flower being so small, yet so perfect. Sometimes I feel that Nature takes a special delight in tiny things, making them so absolutely faultless that the most powerful microscope can only reveal more marvels in them. I wonder how many things made by humans could be tested in the same way and prove themselves as perfect.

Well, all those little flowers are attached to the thick stem (or "axis") in pairs. And if you were to start at the bottom of the stalk and with your pencil follow round and round it from one pair to the next, you would see that you were gradually approaching the top; and when you had finished you would find that you had traced out the form of a spiral. So you would say that the flowers were "spirally arranged."

Now, after the flowers come the fruits—and with these I know you are all well acquainted, for they are the famous "Banksia men." They certainly do look fearsome, as a whole lot of woody nuts are buried in a dark mass of what seems to be brown, wiry hair, but which is in reality all that remains of the vividly-coloured flowers.

Each nut holds inside it two seeds which have wings, and it is so anxious about their welfare that it simply refuses to open out and let them escape

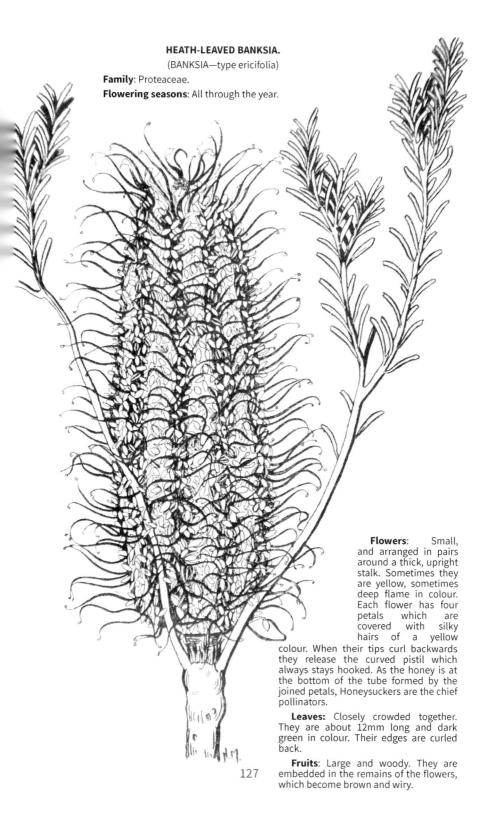

HEATH-LEAVED BANKSIA.
(BANKSIA—type ericifolia)
Family: Proteaceae.
Flowering seasons: All through the year.

Flowers: Small, and arranged in pairs around a thick, upright stalk. Sometimes they are yellow, sometimes deep flame in colour. Each flower has four petals which are covered with silky hairs of a yellow colour. When their tips curl backwards they release the curved pistil which always stays hooked. As the honey is at the bottom of the tube formed by the joined petals, Honeysuckers are the chief pollinators.

Leaves: Closely crowded together. They are about 12mm long and dark green in colour. Their edges are curled back.

Fruits: Large and woody. They are embedded in the remains of the flowers, which become brown and wiry.

into the bush world until a sufficiently dry season arrives. It is because of this that some nuts wait as long as several years before attempting to open.

It is true, I know, that Banksia men used to do dreadful things once upon a time, carrying off poor little fairies and gumnuts and making them captive. But a short time ago, while they were asleep, a few brave fairies came right up to them and brought them a terrible dream which made them feel all the things being done to them that they themselves had done to the little bush folk. And let me tell you a secret: even since that dream, they have been remarkably well-behaved, and at the present time they are even succeeding in making themselves loved amongst the fairies and elves.

Pterostylis Baptistii is always looking down upon me.

The Humble Fairy
(MICROTIS—type porrifolia)

Although I am one of the most humble of Orchids, and hardly ever am I paid any attention by humans, you will find me really very lovely when you look at me closely, for I have such a delicate green colour, mixed with a little white and yellow, and though you may think I am too small to have all the complicated parts in me that my lordlier relations possess, I really have. So just you think what a true masterpiece of Nature I am, when men have to use powerful microscopes (as they call them) to see me properly, yet I am so perfect and complete; and my "labellum" wears the prettiest little scalloped-edged frock, which only a flower-fairy of my size could possibly wear.

I think it must be a definite characteristic of ours to form very strong family affections which make it most difficult for us to part, so you will always see about twenty or more of us on the one stem.

And to make it even better, wherever we decide to settle down we form a real little colony, inhabited by simply dozens of our plants.

This is also very useful because by ourselves we are so small that our friends, the mosquitoes, would not be much impressed with us, and Pterostylis longifolia has explained to you how necessary we find them in our lives.

As it is, however, we look quite beautiful to them, though hardly at all to humans, for at the first glance we are so similar to all the grass in the midst of which we grow. Then, what should we do alone if an enemy should appear? Our tiny forms, you see, make us really quite defenceless, so that it takes a large army of us to be equal to a caterpillar or a snail.

Would you believe it that Pterostylis Baptistii is always looking down upon me, and spreading out her leafy rosette to show me how grand she looks—just because I only happen to have one leaf which is long and narrow? It makes me feel a little peevish at the time, I will admit, but I know it shouldn't, as such behaviour only occurs when we are flowers—when our little material bodies are all we can see; yet at the magic hour when we become fairies—when we become the flower-souls, we cannot help being kind and loving to everyone. We often think human souls must be like that also, but we hardly ever see them to really know.

I should simply love you to come out to the bush and talk to me a little when you have time. I am not very particular about where I live, so you may

MICROTIS—type porrifolia

Family: Orchidaceae.

Flowering season: spring.

Flowers: Green in colour. They are very minute and numerous. The two side sepals are curved backward and the middle one is hooded. The column has two tiny ear-like wings.

The flowers are crowded closely together.

Leaves: Long, smooth and narrow.

Sometimes the plant is extremely small, but other times it may attain a height of one metre. It grows on barren grasslands as well as in swampy regions.

131

come across me almost anywhere from dry, barren hilltops to grassy flats, river banks and quite swampy places.

But I am a real little spring flower! In fact I love spring so much that I always get excited when I know she is approaching. Consequently I come out in bloom in good time to see her make her triumphal entry into the Australian bush.

And now, my small mortal friend, the magic hour is over.

Once more we must arrange ourselves up and down swaying stems and become speechless flowers before we are seen by the eyes of day. Slowly, slowly, I see all my fairy companions drifting away, so, from all the shy bush-flowers who have spoken to you tonight, I say

"GOOD-BYE"

Good-Bye

The shades of night where fairies dwell
Are floating now beyond the trees
And ferns and flowers, across whose eyes
There sweeps a quiv'ring breeze.

And little swaying stems that stood
All unadorned through night's deep hours,
Are holding now, as Dawn awakes,
Some timid bushland flowers!

The witchery of shadows and
The magic spell of dreams have fled;
The bush was filled with fairies—now,
'Tis filled with flowers instead!

Diagram of a Flower (cut down in half)

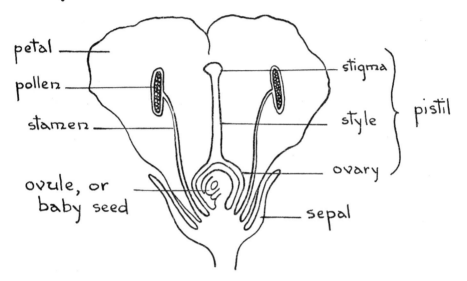

petal
pollen
stamen

ovule, or
baby seed

stigma
style
ovary
sepal

pistil

Printed in Great Britain
by Amazon

38031896R00078

Jan van Impe

The University Library of Leuven
of Leuven

Historical Walking Tour

Lipsius Leuven

First edition published: 2006
Second revised edition: 2012

Lipsius Leuven is an imprint of Leuven University Press

© 2012 Universitaire Pers Leuven / Leuven University Press / Presses
Universitaires de Louvain
Minderbroedersstraat 4, B-3000 Leuven

ISBN 978 90 5867 925 3
D/2012/1869/50
NUR: 693

Translation: Communicationwise

CONTENTS

CONCISE BIBLIOGRAPHY   **103**

APPENDIX: LIST OF COMMEMORATIVE PLAQUES, COMMEMORATIVE STONES AND INSCRIPTIONS ON THE WALLS AND PILASTERS OF THE UNIVERSITY LIBRARY   **107**

PREFACE

This guide to the 'University Library' of the KU Leuven came about at the request of the *Friends of the University Library* and the many visitors to this remarkable building.

The University Library as a whole consists of the Central Library located at Mgr. Ladeuzeplein and the diverse departmental and faculty libraries. Indeed, at the end of 2002, with the opening of the new Campus Arenberg Library in the former Celestine Monastery of Heverlee, a new jewel was added to the crown of the University Library. In this booklet, the name 'University Library' will refer only to the Central Library, since for historical reasons and in the eyes of outsiders, this building today symbolises all the libraries together.

This building is not only a modern scientific library, with paper and digital collections consulted by more than 100,000 readers each year. It is also a major historic monument, whose foundations are anchored in one of the most tragic episodes of the 20th century: the First World War. Moreover, it welcomes visitors from all over the world throughout the year. These visitors would like to know its history and understand what they are seeing during their walk in and around the library.

Part I contains a historic overview of the period 1914-1968: the dramatic fire of August 1914 in the old University Library, then located in the current Universiteitshal along Naamsestraat, the opening in July 1928 of the new University Library at Mgr. Ladeuzeplein, the equally dramatic fire of May 1940 and its reconstruction after the Second World War. The history of the old University Library (1636-1914) is treated in Part II. This might appear to be illogical, but what follows below will show that the fire of 1914 was a crucial event that led directly to the building of the present library. Part III of this book consists of a practical guidebook. Finally, a list of all inscriptions on the building, as well as the texts on the diverse commemorative plaques and the bells can be found in an appendix.

The publication of this booklet took place in conjunction with two extraordinary events. In 2003, the University commemorated the 75th anniversary of the current library building, and in 2003, the Alma Mater also celebrated completion of the restoration work that was begun in October 1999.

Finally, I would like to thank Professor Jan Roegiers and Mark Derez (University Archives), Chris Coppens (Tabularium, Central Library) and Professor Jo Tollebeek for their many suggestions and critical reading of the manuscript. I would also like to thank Professor Andries Welkenhuysen for a number of useful suggestions and for his translations of the numerous Latin inscriptions. And of course I cannot forget Roger Tavernier and Staf Kamers, who were always prepared to share with me their detailed knowledge of the building.

Welcome.

Jan van Impe

ABOUT THE SECOND EDITION

In 2006, an English translation was published of the first Dutch edition of 2003, with a number of textual corrections and a new photo of the letter balustrade that had been repaired in the meantime (p. 83). These are also included in this edition. This second edition of 2012, being published simultaneously with the republication of the Dutch edition, has been corrected and augmented where necessary, and provided with new photos.

Jan van Impe

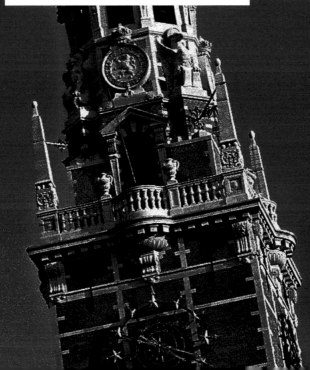

PART I
FROM AUGUST 1914
TO MAY 1968

THE SACKING OF LOUVAIN

LEUVEN BURNS

27 August 1914. The diplomatic representative of the United States of America in Belgium, Brand Whitlock (1869-1934), received a visit in Brussels from Mgr. Jules de Becker (1857-1936), rector of the American College of Louvain. At that moment, the time-honoured university city had already been subject to plundering and looting by German troops for a number of days. The rector was brought to Brussels as a hostage and was released through the intervention of Whitlock. De Becker thanked him – so recounts Whitlock in his Belgian war memoirs published after the war – and told without visible emotions of the terror that took place before his eyes: the houses of his father and brother set on fire, friends and colleagues murdered, civilians executed or deported, Saint Peter's Church gone up in flames.

Relief that was on the war Monument on the Martelarenplein until 1940 and that was restored in 2003. The German army (l.) killing innocent civilians, represented by a lamb. The population flees (m.). The Belgian army resists (r.) (photo: Department of Monuments and Landscapes).

The University Hall was also burnt down, he said. 'The libr … '
There was a pause. He bit his lip and attempted to speak the word
again. 'The lib …' He then placed his arms on the table, dropped
his head and burst into tears. The University Library that, since its
creation in 1636, had been located in the University Hall, was now
a blackened ruin.

On 4 August 1914, the German army invaded neutral Belgium,
which had refused free passage to French territory, without expect-
ing any resistance. The reality of the situation, however, was much
different. The Belgian army indeed resisted and – to the dismay of
the enemy – also made use of guerilla tactics. The forts of Liege
resisted the Germans for a time, falling only after the arrival of
extra heavy 420-mm artillery from Austria. The Belgian army and
government retreated to the ring of forts around Antwerp, from
where on 24 and 25 August an attack was launched in the direction
of Mechelen, Vilvoorde, Hofstade and Haacht in order to lessen
the south-western pressure of the German army on the French
and British troops. This was successful. German divisions advanced
to the north and rushed to the aid of their colleagues. Both sides
suffered heavy losses. The German army was even driven back at a
number of places. The Belgian army approached Leuven to within
a few kilometres, and in the city terrified civilians and nervous
German soldiers - who had occupied Leuven since 19 August -
clearly heard the din of war. After the battle, on the evening of 25
August, shots were fired in the approaching darkness. The German
soldiers present in Leuven mistook each other – or a retreating
German division – for Belgians and began to fire in panic on the
so-called invaders. A number of Germans were killed or wounded.
To cover up this military blunder, the decision was taken to place
the blame on the inhabitants of Leuven. Bloody revenge was then

taken on imagined civil snipers (franc-tireurs), because according to the prevailing law of war (the Conventions of The Hague) and the convictions of the Prussian nobility, no armed resistance should be mounted once the territory was occupied.

The German fury raged through the streets for four days. The city was subjected to plundering and murder. Public, private and university buildings were destroyed with explosives, fuel and phosphorus tablets.

Approximately one ninth of all Leuven buildings were destroyed. 209 civilians were shot down individually or in groups. 650 civilians were deported to Germany in railway cattle cars. Others were driven across the surrounding countryside for days as hostages and mistreated. On 27 August, the population of the city was even driven out after the threat by the German command to reduce Leuven to ruins with targeted artillery shelling. However, it did not come to this.

A German officer declared to the first secretary of the American Embassy Hugh S. Gibson (1883-1954), who on 28 August risked his own life with a visit to burning Leuven: 'We shall make this place a desert. We shall wipe it out so that it will be hard to find where Louvain used to stand. For generations people will come here to see what we have done, and it will teach them to respect Germany and to think twice before they resist her. Not one stone on another, I tell you –*Kein Stein auf einander!*.'

The University Library was also affected: no stone, so to speak, remained unturned. Around 300,000 books, 800 incunabula, 1,000 manuscripts, a part of the University archives - containing among others the original charter of the University from 1425 – and invaluable collections of coins and medals, paintings and sculptures were lost forever. According to a witness in a post-war newspaper, it rained fragments of burned pages as far as Walloon-Brabant.

The Leuven drama was not an isolated incident. Previously places such as Andenne (20-21 August), Tamines (21 August), Aarschot (22 August) and Dinant (23 August) fell victim to this strategy of terrorising the civilian population according to the unfortunately still employed formula of Prussian general Karl von Clausewitz (1780-1831). With this strategy, the German command hoped to demoralise the population and to break the back of the Belgian military resistance. The Germans for that matter had crossed the border with the spectre of wildly shooting Belgian civilians, stirred up by 'infamous' priests. During the first weeks of the war, a false report appeared in the *Kölnische Zeitung* and the Viennese *Freie*

Leuven 1914. The Old Market, with the ruins of the former University Library in the middle to the right (photo: University Archives).

Presse that German and Austrian civilians in - then not yet occupied - Antwerp and Ostend were molested and murdered. Even the graves of German and Austrian compatriots had not been spared. Together with the unexpected opposition of the Belgian army and the resulting losses on German side, all of this brought about a highly explosive atmosphere.

The answer of Belgium to Germany's ultimatum. Political cartoon in Pourquoi Pas? *of 13 August 1914 (photo: University Library).*

INTERNATIONAL INDIGNATION

The Germans had counted on a deterrent effect. They had hoped to command respect in the occupied country as well as in international public opinion. They, however, had miscalculated considerably. National and international indignation with respect to _Le Sac De Louvain_ was great. Reactions from the press illustrate this amply. _The Times_ appeared with the headline:

'Louvain in ashes. Terrible act of German vandalism. (…) A town of 45,000 inhabitants, the intellectual metropolis of the Low Countries since the 15th century, is now no more than a heap of ashes.' (August 29th 1914)

'The burning of Louvain. A crime against humanity. (…) An act without parallel in the history of civilised peoples.' (August 30th 1914)

Sir Arthur Evans (1851-1941), discoverer of Minos' palace on Knossos (Crete), declared in a letter to the editor in the same newspaper:

'Sir, may I be allowed to voice the horror and profound indignation at the Prussian holocaust (sic) of Louvain. (…) This sin against history and against posterity can never, indeed, be condoned

(…) The holocaust of Louvain should at least have the effect of electrifying all the more intellectual elements of our country with a new vigour of determination to overthrow the ruthless regime of blood and iron imposed by the Prussian arrogance on 20th century Europe' (September 1st 1914)

Dutch newspapers responded as follows:

'Leuven Destroyed. (…) It is certain that among the destroyed buildings are the halls of the University with its inestimably rich library that is unique in Europe. (…) It is a punishment that extends farther than the population of Leuven, farther than ravaged Belgium. It is a chastisement that affects all of Western civilisation that exists on this earth.'
(_De_ Nieuwe _Rotterdamsche Courant_, 29 August 1914)

'The destruction of Leuven. (…) However, the conquering people have blemished their name as civilised nation by destroying in blind rage, without any trace of self control, monuments of civilisation, artwork, from a very distinguished past.'

(Prof. C.L. Dake, *De Telegraaf*, 30 August 1914)

The French press also protested:

'The burning of Leuven. Cardinal Mercier. Rome, 30 August. – When Cardinal Mercier, archbishop of Mechelen, learned of the atrocities committed by the Germans in Leuven and Mechelen, he was so upset that he lost consciousness.'

(*Journal des Débats politiques et littéraires*, 1 September 1914)

'It is quite certain that no right of reprisal can justify the devastating fury of the Teutonic troops.'

(*Journal des Débats politiques et littéraires*, 12 September 1914)

The Belgian press, of course, also reacted with shock:

'Leuven destroyed by the Germans. The Germans who shot at each other claim that the people of Leuven attacked them, and they destroyed the city.'

(*De Nieuwe Gazet*, 30 August 1914)

'German fury in Leuven. Major crimes by a Civilised People.'

(*De Gazet van* Antwerpen, 31 August - 1 September 1914)

'The Vandals destroy Leuven. They got drunk, fought each other and are making the people pay for their blunder. The Germans must surely be crazy.'

(*De Volksgazet*, 31 August 1914)

'The attack on Leuven. New American protest.'

(*La Métropole*, 3 September 1914)

'The speech of [British prime minister] Asquith in Guildhall: (…) the greatest crime against civilisation and science since the Thirty Years' War (…)'

(*La Métropole*, 6 September 1914)

The impressive headline in De Volksgazet *(photo: Antwerp Municipal Library).*

The war, which until then was viewed principally as a political-military conflict, suddenly changed into a real battle of cultures. The Leuven bloodbath, the senseless attack on the venerable university city and especially the destruction of the library quickly led to strong reactions. Leuven became the symbol of the wrong-headedness of the German aggressor – with the photos of the burnt-out library as sinister icon – and the concepts *civilisation* and *Kultur* were placed in direct opposition. Indeed, after the armistice one could read an inscription (chronogram)[1] on the scorched facade of the old library: ICI fInIt La CVLtVre aLLeManDe (translation: *Here German culture ceases to exist*). The fate of the Leuven library took

---

1. Chronograms are inscriptions in which the capitalised letters indicate a year according to the Roman system. To this end the 'Roman numerals' in the text are totalled: M = 1.000; D = 500; C = 100; L = 50; X = 10; V = 5; I = 1. Thus we read here the year 1914.

on mythical proportions and it was compared to that of the great library of Alexandria.

Leuven became, in the words of contemporary German historian Wolfgang Schivelbusch, the Sarajevo of the European intelligentsia. Thus on 29 August 1914, the French writer and later Nobel Prize Winner Romain Rolland (1866-1944) published an open letter to Nobel Prize Winner Gerhart Hauptmann (1862-1946), the figurehead of German language and literature, in which he asked him to distance himself from German militarism. Rolland also despairingly asked himself whether Hauptmann should from now on consider himself the heir to Goethe or to Attila the Hun. Hauptmann did not flinch and answered that the Germans would then prefer to continue as the sons of Attila.

The Germans stubbornly refused to admit any guilt. The Leuven population was accused of being incited by the Belgian government to revolt in order to support the Belgian army's sortie from the forts of Antwerp. In so doing, civilians would have committed atrocious crimes against the German soldiers and they were rightly punished for this. On 11 October 1914, 93 German artists, scientists and scholars, including of course Hauptmann, signed an emotional manifesto, the infamous *Aufruf an die Kulturwelt*, which was published in all German newspapers in support of the German version of the facts. Among them were famous names such as scientists and Nobel Prize Winners Wilhelm von Röntgen (1845-1923) and Max Planck (1858-1947), archaeologist and Leuven honorary doctor 1908 Wilhelm Dörpfeld (1853-1940), theatre maker Max Reinhardt (1873-1943), painter Max Liebermann (18471935), historian Karl Lamprecht (1856-1915), philosopher and psychologist Wilhelm Wundt (1832-1920) and Adolf von Harnack (1851-1930), director of the Royal Library in Berlin. According to them, German

Leuven 1914. The burnt-out great hall of the old University Library (photo: University Archives).

culture cannot survive without militarism, a position that had also been defended by Prussian general and war historian Friedrich von Bernhardi (1849-1930) in his bestseller *Deutschland und der nächste Krieg* published in 1913.

The Belgian episcopacy called upon the bishops of Germany and Austria-Hungary to open their eyes to the facts. The cardinals of Cologne and Munich reacted by indignantly complaining to the kaiser about this 'slander concerning the German fatherland and its glorious army.' The freemasons in both camps also faced off. The grand master of the Belgian freemasons proposed that the nine German grand lodges organise a meeting of all grand lodges from the neutral countries in order to prevent 'horrors that all civilised people regret from occurring again'. Most did not answer. The lodges of Bayreuth and Darmstadt, however, did: they praised the indisputable discipline of the German army and the humane way in which, according to them, Germany was conducting the war.

German Kaiser Wilhelm II (1859-1941) even found it necessary to send a telegram to American President Woodrow Wilson (1856-1924) in which he expressed his regret for the fate of Leuven, and as excuse argued that atrocities on the part of priests and women were the cause. However, it was of no avail. The facts were clear; there were too many witnesses. These included the Swiss Albert Félix Füglister (1884-1951), who in 1916 published his eyewitness report in book form, *Louvain. Ville Martyre*, and Dutch war correspondent from *De Tijd*, Lambertus Mokveld (1890-1968), who,

Death presents the German Kaiser with an honorary doctorate amid the ruins of the old University Library. Political cartoon by Albert Pieter Hahn (1871-1918), published in De Notenkraker, *1914 (photo: University Archives).*

also in 1916, published a book with his journalistic observations, *De overweldiging van België*.

The German government also responded, and on 10 May 1915 issued its infamous white paper on the Leuven question. The soldiers would not only have been subject to gun and machine gun fire, but also to boiling oil, even raging women with knives to poke out the eyes of the victims and castrate them. The bitter discussions over the matter would drag on for decades. Only after the end of the Second World War would the Belgian version of the facts officially be accepted.

26

INTERNATIONAL AID

An especially important clause for Leuven was included in the Treaty of Versailles (28 June 1919). Article 247 of the treaty reads as follows: 'Germany undertakes to furnish to the University of Louvain, within three months after a request made by it and transmitted through the intervention of the Reparation Commission, manuscripts, incunabula, printed books, maps and objects of collection corresponding in number and value to those destroyed in the burning of the Library of Louvain' by Germany.

Vignette in a book returned in restitution by Germany (photo: University Library).

However, there had also been earlier initiatives, amid the atmosphere of indignation, to rebuild the library. The Institut de France took the lead already in 1914. It launched the *Oeuvre Internationale pour la reconstitution de l'Université de Louvain*, with as Secretary General, Pierre Imbart de la Tour (1860-1925). During a solemn meeting in Le Havre on 26 August 1918, four years to the day after the fire, this committee received an official character. No less than 239 institutions from the allied countries joined.

The prominent figures who were present gave grandiloquent speeches. Many written expressions of support from prominent individuals were also sent. Thus Field Marshal Douglas Haig (1861-1928), commander-in-chief of the British army in France, wrote: 'That splendid building had stood for many hundred years as the symbol of Art and Learning. Its destruction is the symbol of what we are fighting for.' Field Marshal Ferdinand Foch (1851-1929), commander-in-chief of the allied armies in France, believed: 'This meeting is clear proof of the irreconcilable aversion that the human conscience harbours against barbarian powers.'

Others agreed. Henri Bergson (1859-1941), philosopher and member of the Académie française, declared: 'One of the temples of thought in Belgium has been destroyed.' Nicholas Murray Butler (1862-1947), chair of Columbia University, sent a telegram: 'The whole civilized world was shocked. Modern history might be searched in vain for parallel to this act of wanton brutality and destructiveness.' George Henry Nettleton (1874-1959) of Yale University and chair of the *American University Union*, told his listeners : 'That which Germany is destroying, in reality, is not Louvain but Germany herself.'. Simon Deploige (1868-1927), chair of the Leuven Institute of Philosophy, copiously thanked those present and said that 'the ashes of our library have a symbolic value, like the debris of the cathedral of Reims, like the wreck of the sunken Lusitania'.

It was not limited to written and spoken expressions of support. Books were also donated, first of all in occupied Belgium. Each province established a support committee and began to collect books. The municipal library of Antwerp took the lead. Already on 17 September 1914, during the ongoing siege of Antwerp by the German army, it set aside a batch of books. It was an initiative of head librarian Emmanuel de Bom (1868-1953).

While the university remained closed during the war, considerable work was done on rebuilding the collections. The books received temporary quarters at Saint Gertrude Abbey, Justus-Lipsius College and the Spoelberch Institute. Etienne van Cauwenbergh (1890-1964), appointed as head librarian in 1919, received the difficult task of organising the building up of the new library collections.

Louis Stainier (1870-1935), an experienced librarian with the Royal Library in Brussels, ensured that the book deliveries from Germany prescribed in the Treaty of Versailles actually arrived in Leuven.

Abroad, efforts were made to outdo one another. The Netherlands, France, Great Britain, Denmark, Spain, Italy, Poland, Sweden, Czechoslovakia and Canada collected books for Leuven on a large scale. Greece sent casts of antique sculptures. The American Susan Minns (1839-1938) donated an important part of her invaluable private library on death and the dance of death. Japanese Crown Prince (later Emperor) Hirohito (1901-1989) visited the ruins of the old library in 1921; The Japanese support committee sent a large batch of books to Leuven despite the fact that Japan itself had just been struck by a severe earthquake. Hirohito also personally donated a splendid vase by top artist Seifû Yohei III (1851-1914).

In June 1919, American President Woodrow Wilson was received in Leuven and was awarded an honorary doctorate.

In 1928, the pyramid of books had grown to around 750,000 volumes. Approximately half of these were purchased in implementation of the Treaty of Versailles. This obligation was initially the source of considerable panic in the German library world. German librarians feared they would have to plunder their own collections in order to deliver the required books and manuscripts. It was finally agreed that Germany would pay the value of the destroyed collections and with this capital (2,000,000 Goldmarks), books were purchased on the German book market, which for that matter was a welcome turn of events for the German book trade during the disastrous 1920s.

Book dealer Anton Hiersemann (1891-1961) from Leipzig received a monopoly on delivering new books. After spending the value of the burnt books and manuscripts, the University was able to keep the rest of the allocated amount, and with it purchased shares at a German bank. The dividends were used for new purchases, until 1943. From 1945, the shares were unblocked and books could again be purchased.

Only in 1971 were the shares sold and the proceeds divided between the two 'new' universities, the Katholieke Universiteit Leuven and the Université Catholique de Louvain.

THE NEW UNIVERSITY LIBRARY:
A GIFT FROM THE AMERICAN PEOPLE

On 3 December 1918, the chair of *The National Committee of the United States for the Restoration of the University of Louvain*, Nicholas Murray Butler (1862-1947) – the later chair of the *Carnegie Endowment for International Peace* (1925-1945) and 1931 Nobel Peace Prize Winner – requested the honour of erecting a new library building in Leuven. On 30 October 1919, subscription was opened for 500,000 dollars. To stimulate donations, it was announced that the names of the donors would be immortalised by inscriptions on the walls and the pillars of the new library (see appendix).

The American Committee did not waste any time. The American Whitney Warren (1864-1943), the well-known architect of the impressive Grand Central Terminal in New York, was given the task of designing a new library building. He visited Leuven at the beginning of 1921 in order to select a suitable building site. He eyed with interest a lot between the Volksplaats (the present Mgr. Ladeuzeplein), Arendstraat, Ravenstraat and Blijde-Inkomststraat. A conflict then ensued with the province and the city government, which wanted to construct a new courthouse on the site, but the matter was finally settled.

On 28 July 1921, a hot summer day, the foundation stone was laid at the corner of the Volksplaats and Blijde-Inkomststraat. Joseph Désiré Cardinal Mercier (1851-1926) blessed the stone. Nicholas Murray Butler, who was awarded an honorary doctorate the same day, was given the honour of symbolically laying it. He scooped the cement out of a bucket wrapped in *stars and stripes*. Rector Paulin Ladeuze (1870-1940) was of course present, as were a string of important guests from the political, diplomatic, academic and ecclesiastical world. Among them were the Belgian royal couple Albert I (1875-1934) and Elisabeth (1876-1965), Prince Albert I of Monaco (1848-1922), French Field Marshal Philippe Pétain (1856-1951), then not yet under a cloud, and Raymond Poincaré (1860-1934), ex-president of the French Republic and honorary chair of the French support committee, who ended his speech with the words: 'We begin with the reconstruction of the Leuven library; let us also provide humanity a house with strong foundations!'

On 17 July 1923, the Blijde-Inkomststraat wing together with a part of the book repository was inaugurated. Cardinal Mercier blessed the building and Prince Leopold (1901-1983), the later Leopold

President Wilson (m.) giving a speech among the ruins of the old University Library, in the presence of King Albert I (r.) and Queen Elisabeth (l.). Queen Elisabeth is flanked by the daughter of the president, King Albert I by the first lady. (photo: University Archives).

Nicholas Murray Butler (second from the r.) lays the foundation stone (photo: University Archives).

III, placed the first book on the racks, a commemorative volume containing the names of 196 students killed during the war. At the end of 1924, a temporary reading room and catalogue room were opened. In the meantime, however, funding for the building had come to a halt. The funds collected were insufficient and work was stopped. The ministering angel was Herbert Hoover (1874-1964), later president of the United States (1929-1933), who launched an appeal in his own name. This yielded approximately 300,000 dollars. Hoover was also chair of the *Commission for Relief in Belgium Educational Foundation*, and this commission donated another 350,000 dollars. With this money, the library could be completed. On 4 July 1928, *Independence Day*, it was finally finished. During a ceremony with numerous Belgian and foreign representatives from the academic, religious and political world, the American library was inaugurated. The multitudinous public welcomed Prince Leopold and Princess Astrid (1905-1935), Ernest-Joseph Cardinal van Roey (1874-1961), the Belgian bishops, members of the diplomatic corps, all on a grandstand located in the middle of the square. Van Roey, assisted by Belgian and American bishops, blessed the building, the clock and the carillon, and thanked in detail all those who made the rebirth of the library possible. He made special mention of the American people: 'Each stone gives evidence of the friendship of a citizen, student or child from the United States; each brick will continue to say to each generation that an American hand has laid them in this building.'

American Ambassador Hugh S. Gibson (1883-1954), who had just received an honorary doctorate from the University, has the honour of handing over the golden keys of the new library to rector Ladeuze. He was applauded loudly; those present shouted at the tops of their voices: 'Long live America!'

The festivities were disrupted only once. A low-flying airplane dropped leaflets above the square containing the infamous text: '*Furore Teutonico diruta, dono Americano restituta*' *('Cut down by Teutonic violence, repaired with American generosity')*. Architect Warren had proposed including this text as inscription on the balustrade of the facade. The letters had already been chiselled and partially delivered in Leuven. In the end, Rector Ladeuze did not grant his permission for inclusion of the inscription. In the meantime, the Locarno Peace Conference (1925) after all had brought about a normalisation of relations with Germany, and the rector foresaw problems in the longer term with such a rabid anti-German inscription. He also believed that this text would stand in the way of relations with the German academic world, which would only be a disadvantage to Leuven. Moreover, as an anonymous reader in *La Libre Belgique*

The original Main Reading Room, from before the fire of May 1940 (photo: University Archives

sneered, the Germans would probably decipher the dog Latin used in the inscription with twinkling eyes.

Ladeuze's refusal, however, was a source of considerable commotion. The sculptor of the letters, Pierre de Soete (1886-1948), protested fiercely. Architect Warren even initiated legal proceedings against the University, with an appeal to artistic freedom. The part of the population that could not forget the war atrocities also made their voices heard. The simple balustrade that was installed without text was in fact destroyed three times.

A number of the letters (5) of the second part of the inscription disappeared in the cellars of the town hall. In 1936, very much to the displeasure of Berlin, the first part moved to a war monument in Dinant, which was expertly blown up in May 1940 by the Wehrmacht because it was considered an insult to the German army. Remnants of the second part of the infamous letter balustrade can be viewed today at the Tower Courtyard of the University Library.

The leaflet incident did not spoil the mood for most – the audacious pilot was arrested immediately after landing – and all the guests enjoyed the festive banquet in the Main Reading Room. There was some displeasure heard among the Flemish who believed that too much French was used during the ceremony. Emmanuel de Bom, head librarian of the Municipal Library of Antwerp, was also unhappy. His initiative, as early as September 1914, to present books to Leuven was completely ignored so many years later. He received no official invitation, was not allowed to enter the library and, according to a journalist, was pushed aside by the people.

During the banquet, the radio broadcasted concerts from the most important Belgian carillons. After the meal, the country's carilloneur Jef Denijn (1862-1941) provided festive music on the library carillon. The carillon together with the tower clock was a gift from the American engineers associations, as a tribute to their colleagues killed during the First World War. Denijn played among others 'My old Kentucky home, good night' and 'Columbia the gem of the Ocean' by American songwriter Stephen Foster (1826-1864), the Walloon song 'Leyiz mi plôrer' by Nicolas Defrêcheux (1825-1874) and 'Heeft het roosje milde geuren' by Flemish composer Peter Benoit (1834-1901). In between, the Liege Legia Choir sang serious and less serious songs. The day was concluded with fireworks lighting up the tower.

AMERICA'S GIFT
TO BELGIUM

The Proposed New
Louvain Library

"The plans and drawings all . . . . . are perfect.
Your project has a character eminently practical.
All the different departments are provided for, and
you have solved the various problems which arose
therefrom with an elegant simplicity."

—D. J. CARDINAL MERCIER

To restore a shrine of learning wantonly
destroyed

To provide Belgium's greatest University
with a working library

To immortalize America's homage to
heroic defense of liberty

GIVE TO THE MILLION DOLLAR
LOUVAIN RESTORATION FUND

THE FIRE OF MAY 1940

Fourteen years after those dramatic days of August 1914, the academic community was able to breathe a sigh of relief. It had a modern library – built in neo-Flemish renaissance style, and showered with reminders of the allied victory – equipped according to the most recent insights of the American library world, as these were applied among others at the famous New York Public Library. The reading room was located in front, the book repository at the rear, with in between the catalogue room as well as offices and seminar rooms in the wings. The floors of the book repository were made of glass concrete in order to increase fire safety. In 1940, the racks contained more than 900,000 volumes and there was room for 300 readers in the Main Reading Room. In other words, the University of Leuven could boast a major scholarly library. Until 1940, it lent out more publications to the other Belgian universities than it requested from them. At that moment, the library again had at its disposal a respectable collection of manuscripts and early printed works.

Then the Second World War erupted. Belgium was neutral, but Germany invaded the country on 10 May 1940. The manuscripts and incunabula had already been safely stored in the bombproof and fireproof cellars of the library in September of 1939. During the initial days of the war, the catalogues, the registers and the reference

America's gift to Belgium. Brochure advertising for the 'Million Dollar Louvain Restoration Fund'. An appeal was made to the generosity of the American citizen, using among others this argument: 'As France gave to America the Statue of Liberty in tribute to our service to the world freedom in the Revolutionary War, so, let us give to Belgium the Louvain Library in gratitude for the inspiration which her heroic defense of liberty in the World War has been to all mankind.' (photo: University Archives).

Leuven 1940. The burnt-out University Library, as photographed by Edgard Vandeven of Leuven (photo: University Archives).

library were brought to safety. There were good reasons to be concerned. Leuven after all was located on a line of defence, the so-called Koningshooikt-Waver line. British and French troops came to the aid of Belgium. The German columns, however, advanced quickly and reached Leuven on 14 May 1940; Leuven had already been bombed by the Luftwaffe on 10 May. Belgian and British units, under the command of Major General Bernard Law Montgomery (1887-1976), fiercely defended their positions, among others with heavy artillery shelling. Their efforts were in vain, as their forces were outnumbered. The French troops close to Dinant and Sedan were trampled by German General Erwin Rommel (1891-1944), the later Desert Fox, and retreated to France. On 16 and 17 May, the Belgian and British soldiers abandoned Leuven.

The unthinkable happened. The new library was completely burnt out. Only 15,000 volumes – including the books donated by Japan – of the more than 900,000 volumes, as well as fifteen manuscripts survived the disaster. The fire was so intense that the repository floors of glass concrete melted. The paste flowed like lava into the cellars and there destroyed the precious works and part of the collection of antique coins. The three illuminated manuscripts that were on loan in August 1914, and thus survived the first fire, were also destroyed. Only a few rooms, the walls, the tower, the tower clock and the carillon survived the inferno.

The cause of this second fire continues to be a source of discussion until today. In August 1914, the Leuven population itself and many foreigners were eyewitnesses to the arson. On 10 May 1940, however, a part of the Leuven population had fled after the bombing by the Luftwaffe; the rest were evacuated a few days later by the military authorities. Thus, the testimony available was scarce; after the war, it was collected in a report by the *War Crimes Commission*.

On 16 May 1940, witnesses saw German artillery from Kessel-lo and Lovenjoel shoot at the library towers, probably because the tower had strategic value as a potential observation post. Or was there a deliberate attempt, i.e. with a special commando unit, to destroy an anti-German monument, among other things under the faulty assumption that the infamous letter balustrade decorated its facade? Afterwards, twelve grenade impact points were counted on the building, chiefly on the tower, the balustrade of which also partially destroyed. Fragments from German 77-mm artillery were found on the inner courtyards. It is possible that the library was also hit by one or more bombs dropped from German aircraft, as stated by another witness. It is still not certain whether all of this caused the fire, especially because it has not yet been established whether the fire spread from above to below as a result of a grenade hit on the roof of the repositories, or that it originated in the cellar due to an unknown cause. Indeed, an enormous explosion took place in the cellar that left a large crater in the floor above it. In any case, the fire was first noticed by a monk at Keizersberg Abbey on 17 May, at 3 a.m. Extinguishing the fire was not possible because the water supply to the city had failed.

Once again, the repositories burned and smouldered for days. Books are tough, and burn slowly. German chemist Karl Keller-mann (1893-?) was appointed as expert. The blame was originally shifted to the retreating British troops. They would have set the library on fire using petrol in order to again portray the Germans as uncultured barbarians.

This accusation appeared in the German press and in a number of Belgian collaboration newspapers. It was so grotesque and implausible, however, that a second investigator was appointed, court martial committee member Henning Freiherr von Beust (1892-1965),

Goebbels (second from l.) before the burnt-out University Library (photo: University Archives).

a military judge. It seems he laughed off the assertion of Keller-mann. The results of his investigation, however, were never published, and no trace of the report has been found to this day. The appointment of a second investigator, however, proves that the German government took the matter very seriously. In addition, no less a person than Joseph Goebbels (1897-1945), Reichsminister für Volksaufklärung und Propaganda and notorious book burner, came to inspect the ruins at the moment when Adolf Hitler (1889-1945) was visiting Paris in triumph (23 June 1940). After his inspection, Goebbels expressed the wish to take a number of burned books with him. The Germans probably feared another worldwide reaction. The Second World War, however, was a different war. This time the destruction did not generate the same response.

THE RECONSTRUCTION

Frankfurt librarian Richard Oehler (1878-1948) – nephew of Friedrich Nietzsche – who in 1920 was appointed as state commissioner for the reconstruction of the Leuven library destroyed in 1914, received another assignment from the German government in 1940. He was to write a report on the burnt-out library, estimate the value of the lost books and develop a future plan for the University Library. He proposed presenting the British with the bill after the war. They would be required to pay as much as the Germans did in implementation of the Treaty of Versailles. Moreover, Oehler advised building a completely new, ultramodern library as a symbol of the victory over the allies. Nothing ever came of this. The University borrowed money, a temporary roof was installed to limit the water damage, and that was it. Only after the liberation could the restoration be started.

Head librarian Etienne van Cauwenbergh was given the task of building up new collections a second time. The American College, located along the Naamsestraat, was set up as temporary library. Strangely enough, the Germans also resumed their pre-war book deliveries until 1943. Book dealer Hiersemann for that matter visited the ruins and was much moved. He knew all too well the value of the lost collections, a large part of which he himself had delivered within the framework of the Treaty of Versailles. Leuven, however, was again able to count on national and - albeit to a lesser degree than after the First World War - international solidarity. In addition, the university, in contrast to the period 1914-1918, was not closed and the professors and students of course urgently required study material.

In Belgium, 28 municipal and regional aid committees were set-up. There were personal donations, but also libraries – such as the Royal Library, the University Library of Gent and the Municipal Library of Antwerp – and a variety of cultural institutions displayed their love of books. The flow increased quickly and was collected in some fifty depots that were regularly emptied with the help of the library lorry.

No place did more than Brussels. Students walked the streets and collected the books from houses with pushcarts. Financial donations quickly followed as well, among others from the *National Fund for Scientific Research*; these were used to pay for a new reference library and subscriptions.

Head librarian Mgr. Etienne van Cauwenbergh (photo: University Archives).

After a short period, the library lorry was requisitioned. Rector Honoré van Waeyenbergh (1891-1971) did not become discouraged, however, and personally used his own car to collect books wherever it was needed. After each weekend, the students for their part brought packages of books with them via train and tram.

Van Waeyenbergh was arrested in June 1943 because he refused to hand over the registration lists of students to the occupying forces. The German authorities were looking for people who had refused to engage in obligatory work in Germany, and the Jewish students who had gone into hiding in Leuven after the Brussels University had closed in the meantime. Leuven tobacco producer Van der Elst came to the rescue. The books were picked up by his lorries after the delivery of smoking material and stored at the company.

Purchases in the occupied countries were prohibited after a short time but were secretly continued, and neutral countries were also contacted. Among others, the Netherlands, France, Ireland, America, Great Britain, Switzerland, Portugal and the Scandinavian countries donated books, some of which would only be delivered after the war. The American College quickly began to burst at the seams. From June 1940 to July 1944, around 350,000 volumes received a temporary home there. In 1948, the number of books in Leuven had grown to approximately 500,000 volumes, and in 1958, the threshold of 750,000 was surpassed.

Ex dono from a book donated after 1940 (photo: University Library).

After the liberation in 1944, repair of the library building could finally begin. Brussels architect Henry Lacoste (1885-1968) drew up the plans. The repairs – which except for the exterior walls, the tower, the ground floor and the stairwells amounted in fact to a completely new building – progressed quickly. From 1946 onwards, the first books

44

could be housed in the Main Reading Room, which temporarily served as repository.

Between 1947 and 1949, the Brussels firm *Moens & Cie* rebuilt the repositories. Nine levels with steel racks, concrete floors, safe electrical wiring, fire locks and steel fire doors that closed automatically were installed. The total length of the bookracks came to around 45 km.

In 1950-1951, the firm *Pernet* from Brussels furnished the Main Reading Room. The original barrel vaulting had already been replaced by a flat concrete ceiling, so that space became available for a second gallery in the Main Reading Room itself, and for two extra floors above it. Tons of splendid oak were supplied and incorporated into what now must be one of the most beautiful reading rooms in the country, with room for 260 readers. Sculptor Jacques Moeschal (1913-2004) created the sculptures on the stairwells and the balustrades.

THE SCHISM AFTER 1968

The collection continued to grow spectacularly in the post-war years. It was as if the suffering of the second fire had to be neutralised as quickly as possible. Then came the turbulent 1960s. The political, cultural and economic conflicts between the Dutch speakers and the Francophones became increasingly violent. The battle between the two groups was also fought in the time-honoured university city, not only verbally but also with cobblestones, which proved to be decisive arguments when flying through the air. Here and there genuine Molotov cocktails were also poured. In 1968, the government resigned due to the Leuven question.

The inevitable verdict is issued. From the old, unitary, bilingual body were born two autonomous and independent universities: the Dutch-speaking *Katholieke Universiteit Leuven* and the French-speaking *Université Catholique de Louvain*. The francophones left Leuven and constructed a new university city, Louvain-la-Neuve, in Ottignies, located in Walloon-Brabant.

The new repositories under construction (photo: University Archives).

Both parties demanded their share of the library collections. Of course, one of the two new universities could have been compensated financially, but this solution appeared to be infeasible. The key question suddenly became: how in the name of God does one divide up a scientific library consisting of almost 1,600,000 books? A first batch of books presented few problems. A considerable part of the still relatively new collection after all consisted of donations. The original donors, or their heirs, were contacted and allowed to make the decision. They thus were able to determine whether the donations in their totality remained in Leuven or went to Louvain-la-Neuve. In a number of other cases, Flemish and French-speakers collegially divided collections among themselves. There were of course multiple sets of many journals, series, encyclopaedias and ongoing bibliographies. Here again the division did not present extraordinary problems; each party retained a complete set. Finally, the manuscripts and valuable works were divided according to their market value.

There remained, however, a large quantity of mainly monographs that could not be divided according to the above-mentioned criteria, and an impasse was reached. What allocation formula could one use here? Language? Subject matter? Age? Publisher? In the end, a system as bizarre as it was impartial and efficient was applied, launched in fact as a joke in the weekly *Pourquoi Pas*? The Flemish received the material with odd location numbers while the francophones received the even. This system is also behind many absurd stories that still today are passed on as absolute truth. Each book, each periodical, each encyclopaedia, each series or ongoing bibliography receives a unique location number in the repositories (e.g. B501 or X600), unrelated to the numbering the publisher may have attached to the volumes. Thus, it is not so that encyclopaedias

The division of the University Library. Caricature of Flip, appearing in De Spectator *in 1970 (photo: University Archives).*

and periodical collections were split, and that for example half of an *Encyclopaedia Britannica* was moved to Louvain-la-Neuve.

After this drastic slimming down, an extra – albeit much too small – budget was made available in order to supplement the gaps created in the collections as quickly as possible. This was done partially by microfilming collections that moved to Louvain-la-Neuve. Moreover, the new loss once again provided a particularly strong stimulus to increase the number of books in every possible way: purchase, exchange, donations. These stimuli remain very strong today. The library is still able to rely on countless donations from professors, alumni, sympathisers and a variety of institutions. Finally, already quite early on - in 1977 - the computerised catalogue DOBIS/ LIBIS was put into use, allowing Leuven and Louvain-la-Neuve to present their collections together. The divided library is thus "virtually" reunited. There is also extensive interlibrary loan traffic between the two institutions. In addition, initiatives have been taken recently to intensify collaboration between both libraries.

After the split, the Leuven University Library had around 800,000 volumes on its shelves. Today, 44 years later, there are more than 5,000,000. Moreover, of course the University Library has been

In June of 2001, Rector André Oosterlinck (1946) welcomed first lady Laura Bush (1946) in the Main Reading Room. The link with the USA is still strong. First lady Barbara Bush (1925) also honoured the University Library with a visit in May 1989 (photo: Rob Stevens).

embracing the digital electronic world for some time now. Thus, it offers around 20,000 full text journals online as well as approximately 700 databases and selected websites. With this, the University Library, together with the Albert I Royal Library and the university libraries of Gent and Liege, is one of the largest academic libraries in the country.

PART II
THE OLD UNIVERSITY
LIBRARY 1636-1914

It is 9 December 1425, a quarter of a century before the invention of printing. In Rome, Pope Martin V (1368-1431) signs the foundation charter of the Leuven University. The city government of Leuven and the chapter of Saint Peter have got what they wanted. A prestigious institution such as a university will breathe new life into the time-honoured ducal city of Leuven after the decline of its cloth industry. The young university gets off to a quick start and will be a high point of learning, especially in the sixteenth century. To be sure, a library is set up in 1438 in the Faculty of Arts, but it will be 1636 before the university has a fully-fledged central library at its disposal. During these first two hundred years, there are of course sufficient books and manuscripts present, but they are located at different locations in addition to the aforementioned library. Professors and students make use of monastery libraries, inside and outside the city walls, as well as the smaller collections present in the various colleges and educational institutions in the city. Of course the professors themselves build up small and large private libraries.

However, in 1636 it becomes a fact. The latinist Erycius Puteanus (1574-1646), successor to Justus Lipsius (1547-1606), visits famous libraries, such as the Ambrosiana in Milan, during his sojourn in Italy. He takes initiatives and finally on the top floor of the old cloth makers' hall (Lakenhal) on Naamsestraat – the present Universiteitshal – the old auditorium of the faculty of medicine is equipped as library. On 1 October 1636, the first head librarian, Valerius Andreas (1588-1655), delivers the opening address for the new academic year. He begins with a modest collection of 2,630 titles, books on theology, medicine and mathematics, principally donated by Laurentius Beyerlinck (1578-1627), an Antwerp canon, and Jacobus Romanus (1588-1635), professor of medicine.

The old Lakenhal before August 1914, with the stairs to the library at the rear (photo: University Archives).

After the death of Erycius Puteanus and Valerius Andreas, the library was neglected for a long time. The academic authorities appeared to have little interest. The collection grew only slightly and prior to 1720 had only 4,000 volumes. Then, in 1720, Domien Snellaerts (1650-1720), a canon from Gent, bequeaths his library of 3,600 books to the Leuven library. He, however, imposed a condition that the books must be housed in a respectable location. With this, Snellaerts provided an important impulse, which on 22 April 1723 – during the rectorate of doctor of medicine Hendrik Jozef Rega (1690-1754) – resulted in the foundation stone being laid for a new library located between the former Lakenhal (Universiteitshal) and the Old Market, the present so-called Rega Wing. It opened its doors on 14 March 1725, and was finally completed in 1733.

A beer and wine cellar was located on the ground floor of the building in which professors and students could enjoy tax-free wines and beers. The more they consumed, the better it was for their library, as a part of the proceeds was used to maintain the Rega Wing.

The great hall of the library, in fact a glorified library repository, was located on the second floor, in the room that today is the Promotion Hall, and was accessible from the old medieval Lakenhal via a double staircase.

A large budget was allocated to furnishing this great hall. Henri Bonnet of Nivelles and Denis Georges Bayar (1691-1774) of Namur designed the floor, ceiling and furniture: a splendid parquet floor, ingeniously sculptured and embellished oak library furniture, pictures of the Holy Spirit, Christ and the all-seeing Eye of God, life-size oak statues, inscriptions and symbols from the arts and sciences. A handsome wrought iron gate by Jean Albert Corbeaux

Great hall of the old University Library (photo: University Archives).

provides an extra measure of closure to the access doors. The oak statues depict Homer, Herodotus, Hippocrates, Cicero, Pope Martin V, Pope John IV, Moses, Saint Luke, Saint Thomas, Saint Peter, Saint Augustine, Saint Gregory, Eusebius and Emperor Justinian. The hall is 44 metres long, 9 metres wide and 9 metres high, and is illuminated by 11 large windows. It became a very impressive room, the pride of the university, and was willingly shown to guests of all ranks.

Around this time, however, the number of books had not yet reached 8,000, and it would grow very slowly over the next 40 years, principally due to donations both small and large. The library after all was faced with a chronically insufficient budget, mismanagement and interference from the authorities. A short golden age dawned when in 1772, Jan Frans van de Velde (1743-1823) was appointed as new head librarian. He succeeded in securing the required funding and in a short space of time supplemented the collections, reaching the respectable number of approximately 50,000 volumes. Then fate intervened. The French Revolution erupted and the Austrian Low Countries were annexed by France. In 1795-1797, thousands of rare works were expropriated on behalf of the Republic. The university was closed in 1797; all of its possessions were confiscated. Parts of the library collections were spirited away or simply sold off. The city of Leuven, however, appreciated the value of a library within its walls; in 1800, it took the battered library under its wings.

After the defeat of Napoleon (1769-1821) in Waterloo (1815), the Belgian provinces were part of the Kingdom of the Low Countries for a short time. In 1816, King Willem I (1772-1843) started state universities in Gent, Liege, as well as Leuven. The city of Leuven gave the library to the new university, a new head librarian was

Remnants of a book burnt in 1914, packaged as a relic in a sealed glass case (photo: University Archives).

appointed and a sizeable budget was made available. The library was reorganised and the number of volumes quickly rose to 60,000.

In 1830, however, Belgium separated from the Netherlands and became independent. In 1834, the Catholic University was established in Mechelen as successor and heir to the Old University. It moved to Leuven in 1835 and the state university there was closed. Professor Wilhelm Amadeus Arendt (1808-1865) from Germany, church historian, archaeologist and classicist, became the new head librarian. An important golden age dawned. Not only were many purchases made, but many professors also bequeathed their private libraries. The library was quickly faced with an acute lack of space. Books and journals literally bulged out of the great hall, the auditoria and even the attics. In 1912, Rector Ladeuze finally took a decision. The lecture rooms on the first floor of the Rega Wing were torn down and German technicians from a company based in Leipzig installed metal library furniture during the winter of 1913-1914.

One half year later German troops set fire to the library. Only a few burned pages and a number of completely charred books were recovered. Today they are on display in a glass shrine at the museum (Valerius Andreas Room) of the University Library as paltry relics of an incomprehensible drama.

PART III
GUIDED TOUR

STYLE

The now 84-year-old library building designed by Whitney Warren still evokes mixed reactions. The academic authorities and the citizens of Leuven initially feared that Warren would erect a skyscraper or a neo-Greek temple. Their fears were unfounded. Warren created a nostalgic, historicised building that refers to the glorious past of Belgium from the renaissance and baroque periods. The typically Flemish belfry tower greatly reinforces these references. This neo-style for that matter fits perfectly the Leuven street scene of the 1920s, which was then largely rebuilt in such neo-styles. In a 1928 article on the inauguration, a journalist noted that the building had an unbalanced style. Some today also find that it is an ugly building. Others are misled by the historical look and think that it is an original building from days long past.

The style is inspired by Flemish renaissance architecture from the late 16th century. Paradoxically, an original example on this scale is nowhere to be found in Belgium. This style was popular especially in the Netherlands during the Golden Century, and in Denmark. In particular, Warren used the Danish castle Frederiksborg as model.

Warren supplemented this totality in Flemish neo-renaissance style with diverse symbols and direct references to the First World War and the allied victory, Belgian patriotism and friendship with America. Thus, the building before you is not only a library but also a war monument as well as an impressive symbol of international solidarity and the desire for peace. This remarkable, unique combination is its true strength. The renovation work (1999-2003) has in fact restored the original lively colours of the brick and the stone, emphasised at strategic places by gilding and cheerful polychromy.

The University Library in the 1930s (photo: University Archives).

FACADE

A visit to the University Library is best begun at the middle of Mgr. Ladeuzeplein. This location provides an excellent view of the rectangular building: 71 metres wide, 50 metres deep, and 80.50 metres high. It was constructed in brick from Boom and two types of French limestone: Euville and Savonnières. It looks all the more impressive because the square slopes downward and the building is located at approximately the highest point of the city centre. A large, rather baroque gable - 14 metres wide and 32 metres high - protrudes from the middle. A stone balustrade runs to the left and right of the middle section, divided into 12 sectors by a number of pilasters. On each pilaster is a stone vase that originally contained wrought-iron flowers: the French fleur-de-lis, the Japanese chrysanthemum, the Canadian maple leaf and the rose of York. These flowers symbolised the allies of the First World War. The flower pieces were removed in 1969. Unfortunately, they were thrown out by mistake during the 1970s. The new flower pieces, installed at the beginning of 2003, were made by ornamental metalworker Dirk van der Loeff from Melle. They were modelled after the only original flower that could be found: a French fleur-de-lis. The stalks and leaves are made of stainless steel that has been painted green. The calyces are made of tin-plated copper, the stamens of copper that has been painted yellow. At the centre of the balustrade, you see the American eagle with a sheaf of arrows and an olive branch, and to the right the Belgian coat of arms, both crowned by a stone obelisk.

Your attention is probably first attracted to the central gable. For the regilding of a number of parts, no less than 6,000 sheets of gold leaf were used. In the middle, in a large niche, you see the four and a half metre high statue of Our Lady of Victory with the

The central gable, fully restored in 2002-2003 (photo: JvI).

child Jesus on her left arm. It is a somewhat unorthodox, bellicose representation of Mary that evoked many negative reactions in the 1920s and 30s. She is wearing a WW I soldier's helmet embellished with oak leaves, and a gilded sword pierces a Prussian eagle, on which she confidently places a foot. In traditional, medieval representations, Mary treads on a dragon or a snake, symbol of the devil. In her position and weaponry, we also recognise the ancient goddess Pallas Athena (Minerva), goddess of war, but also goddess of the arts and literature.

The Madonna was designed by celebrated French sculptor Jean Dampt (1854-1945). He also created among others the angels on the bell tower of Sacré-Coeur in Paris. Leuven sculptor Jozef van Uytvanck (1884-1967) executed the work according to his model. For the original gilding of the weaponry (it was recently restored as well), according to a popular but never proven story, a five dollar piece would have been used that was found on the body of a slain American soldier. Above the niche in which Mary is located, you see the coat of arms of the city of Leuven. The side niches contain large ornamental vases.

The middle section around the Madonna is flanked by two saints. On the left, you see a winged Saint George slaying the dragon with a spear, and on the right, a winged Saint Michael raising his sword to kill his dragon. A shining cross is depicted on the shield of Saint Michael. Both courageous dragon slayers have rather traditional heads, almost as if they were ancient heroes. They depict the victory of good over evil. Saint George is here represented with wings, which in fact is nonsense. Only Saint Michael, as archangel, is allowed to go through life with wings. Evidently, the designers indulged in a fantasy here, or perhaps they were less familiar with the 'laws' of Christian iconography.

Jean Dampt with his brainchildren: Our Lady of Victory and the child Jesus (photo: University Archives).

At the very top of the facade you see a bas-relief depicting the burning library on Naamsestraat. This half-elevated sculpture is crowned by a large shell motif and obelisks, and is flanked on the sides by two hermes: left a female, right a male, both with a tail-shaped lower body and wings.

Below the statue of Mary, at the height of the Main Reading Room, are three busts. In the middle, you will recognise King Albert I, as king/soldier, with soldier's helmet, on the left Prince Leopold, the later Leopold III, and on the right, Queen Elisabeth, wife of Albert I.

The ground floor consists of a gallery with 17 arches, finished with sober, wrought-iron fencing. Above this you will notice the floor with the Main Reading Room, which receives ample light via 17

Saint George (photo: JvI).

Saint Michael (photo: JvI).

high, rectangular windows with stone window jambs. The roof has a 60-degree slope and is adorned with three rows of dormers, crowned with wrought-iron finials. The two large chimneys, left and right, are topped off with small obelisks.

On the facade are also various wall clamps with elegant woven letters attached. On the ground floor, at the top between the arches, is UCL, for Universitas Catholica Lovaniensis, and between the first floor and the balustrade appear the crowned letters A and E, for Albert and Elisabeth, the then Belgian royal couple.

We also draw your attention to three important chronograms[2] running along the edge of the arch of the main entrance, and along the arch to its left and its right. On the left you read:

SANGVINIS AMERICI BELGII LIBERATIONIS CAVSA PROFVSI RECORDATIONI PERENNI (1928: *As a lasting memorial to the American blood that was shed for the liberation of Belgium*). Written in the middle is: SIDERVM CONCVRSV PHOENIX RECRESCIT (1928: *When the stars hasten to help, the Phoenix rises again*). And on the left you see: IVRIS SERVATORIBVS ALBERTO MERCIER BELGICAE NATIONI STATVS CONFOEDERATI (1928: *To the defenders of justice Albert and Mercier, to the Belgian people: the United States*).

On the far right, at the corner of Blijde-Inkomststraat, you can admire the foundation stone. On one side you see the American eagle with coat of arms, and the city arms of Leuven, carried by a Belgian lion. On the other side is the chronogram:

+ LAPIS PRIMARIVS BIBLIOTHECAE LOVANIENSIS NOBILITER REFICIENDAE (1921: *Foundation stone for the rebuilding in splendour of the Leuven Library*).

2. See footnote p. 22.

Foundation stone: coats of arms (photo: JvI)

Foundation stone: inscription (Photo: JvI).

In the meantime, you have perhaps admired the more than 300 commemorative stones with the names of the American benefactors: famous universities such as Columbia, Harvard, Berkeley, Yale, Pennsylvania and Princeton, but also ordinary schools for boys and girls. The inscriptions were made in more than 100 different typefaces, and the totality therefore also provides a splendid sampling of calligraphic styles. You will find a complete list of these inscriptions and their location at the end of this guide.

BLIJDE-INKOMSTSTRAAT SIDE

The side of the University Library on Blijde-Inkomststraat, in the vicinity of Herbert Hooverplein, has a stepped gable that is 14.25 metres wide and 30 metres high. It consists of two ground floor arches and two large windows on the first floor. Between these windows, you can see a smaller window with a balcony and a bust of Cardinal Mercier, a work by Brussels sculptor Pierre de Soete

(1886-1948). Between the ground floor arches you also see an inscription in honour of Cardinal Mercier:

*CARDINALIS MERCIER STVDII GEN[ERALIS]
LOVAN[IENSIS] MAG[ISTRI] PRIMATIS BELGII POPVLI
SVI DVCTORIS AC PATRIAE AVSPICIS MEMORIAE
DICATVM.*

*(translation: Dedicated to the memory of Cardinal Mercier, lecturer at
the Leuven University, Primate of Belgium, leader of his people and
visionary of the fatherland.)*

At the top of the facade you see another representation of *Sedes Sapientiae (Seat of Wisdom)*, with the year Ao Di MCMXXVII (1927). The medieval image of a sitting Mary with the child Jesus on her lap, located in Saint Peter's Church, has been the patron saint of the University since 1835 as well as its emblem since 1909. On the steps of the gable you will notice a number of heraldic animals, symbols of the allies of the First World War. From left to right these are the American eagle, the Italian she-wolf, the Belgian lion, the

Japanese lion of Fo (photo: JvI).   *American eagle (photo: JvI).*

British unicorn, the French rooster and the Japanese lion of Fo. The polychromy of the coats of arms has been restored. The facade is crowned by an obelisk.

On the right of this sidewall is a 30-metre high ziggurat, topped by a magnificent weathervane that was restored in 2001 by ornamental metalworker Dirk van der Loeff. The foot of this weathervane is 'supported' by four elegant and playful, gilded sea horses. In the wall below you see a relief containing the year 1914, the city arms of Leuven, a burning torch and a bayonet as a reminder of the destruction of Leuven in August 1914. Identical commemorative stones, but smaller in format, were installed in all the walls of the houses in Leuven that were reconstructed after the war.

The stepped gable at the rear, the side of the book repository, has a simpler design. It is also 14.25 metres wide and 30 metres high. You see two sets of three windows, then one large window, with a smaller window left and right, and finally, one window in the peak. The steps of the gable again contain the 'allied' animals: the Serbian eagle, the Romanian lion, the Russian bear and the Portuguese winged dragon. On the top steps left and right are decorative vases, and all the way at the top, an obelisk.

The indented facade between the two stepped gables is very sober. It contains one row of five windows and two rows of six windows. On the balustrade, there are four vases that originally contained wrought-iron 'allied' flowers. New flower pieces were also installed here at the beginning of 2003. On the supports of the divide between the second and the third floor you see the year 19/23. This was the year in which this part of the library was put into use. Over the entire width of the indented facade, on a strip between the first and the second floor, is the following chronogram: IN FVNEREA NOCTE AMICA COLLVX-ERVNT SIDERA (1928: *During the fatal night shone friendly the stars*). The Stars are of course another of the many references to the United States. The service entrance, from where the books are also loaded and unloaded, is located here. The double wooden gate is dated 1949, the year in which this part of the library was put back into use after the destruction of May 1940.

REAR

The rear of the repository (Ravenstraat) is also very sober and, given the difference in height with respect to Mgr. Ladeuzeplein, is also quite low. The balustrade is interrupted by 9 dormers with cross-shaped window posts. An appropriate chronogram was chiselled into the stone frieze here that extends across the entire width of the building at ground floor height: FACE CONSVMPTA FAXVNIVERSO ACCENDARIS IPSA (1928: *May you who were consumed by the torch of war, yourself be a torch for all the world*).

The Arendstraat side is almost identical to that of the Blijde-Inkomststraat. On the stepped gable of the Main Reading Room, all the way at the top, there is also a large relief depicting *Sedes Sapientiae*. It is dated: *Ao Di MCMXXVII* (1927). Below it you read the following chronogram: SVCCENDERVNT GENTIBVS LVMINAR IN SAECVLA (1928: *For the peoples they lit a beacon for the centuries*). On the steps of the gable, again the allied heraldic animals are sitting proudly . From left to right you see the American eagle, the Italian she-wolf, the Belgian lion, the British unicorn, the French rooster and the Japanese lion of Fo.

Here again the indented facade between the two stepped gables is very sober. The balustrade is interrupted by four dormers with

View of the repositories from Ravenstraat, taken during the 1930s (photo: University Archives).

cross-shaped window posts crowned with an obelisk. On the stepped gable of the book repository are other heraldic animals. Here you recognise: the Romanian lion, the Serbian eagle, the Russian bear and the Portuguese winged dragon.

BELL TOWER

The carillon tower is 73.50 metres high (80.50 metres high including the weathervane).[3] It is located two thirds of the way across the building. The lower, square part of the tower is 9.75 metres wide and 48 metres high. This lower building has four floors, recognisable by their twin windows. The large clock faces are located on the fourth floor. They have a diameter of 4.60 metres, and were made of wrought iron by the French firm *Baguès* after a model of the American sculptor René Paul Chambellan (1893-1955) and according to the design of Warren and Wetmore. The numerals for the hours on the four dials have been replaced by gilded stars, which together symbolise the then 48 states (Alaska and Hawaii joined later) of the United States. These stars were made by H.J. Stehli, former captain of the 11th Engineers and vice-president of the *Sintering Machine Company*, New York. They were made of aluminium bronze donated by William Hastings Bassett (1868-1934), technical director of the *American Brass Company*, Waterbury, Connecticut. The dials and the stars were restored and regilded where needed during the spring of 2001.

The original, traditional metal clock mechanism from 1928, with cogs and pendulum, still functions. It was designed and made by renowned English bell-founders *Gillett & Johnston* from Croydon (London), and from the beginning had an electric drive (i.e. the

3. With thanks to Jos van Lierop (Technical Services KU Leuven).

Spire with sound louvers and angels playing music (photo: JvI).

required energy is not generated by weights). It was modernised in 1983 by the Holsbeek firm *Clock-O-Matic*. Since then, the pendulum no longer moves and a modern quartz clock and a new electric motor drive the original clock mechanism. This quartz clock in turn is calibrated every minute via radio signals from the official German atomic clock in Mainflingen, close to the most important book city in the world, Frankfurt am Main. This atomic clock is accurate to within 1 second per 150,000 years. The switch from summer to winter time is also handled in this way.

Every quarter of an hour, you hear the sounds of a popular Flemish folk song, the 'Reuzegom', according to reports in fact a drinking song. In a city with more than 38,000 students and a world-famous brewery, this should not really be a problem for anyone. Short variations of the song are played on the first and second quarters of the hour, on the third quarter a shortened version of the song itself is played; you can hear the entire version only on the fourth quarter. The drum that plays this tune – driven by an electric motor – does not have adjustable pins. Thus the Reuzegom, based on an idea of Jef Denijn, has been playing for more than 80 years.

The hammer of the large bourdon – *The Liberty Bell of Louvain* – that rings on the hour is activated by a separate mechanism consisting of an electric motor and a flywheel that winds up and releases the spring of this hammer.

The square part of the tower is demarcated by an overhanging cornice, a balustrade and four obelisks. Here begins the peak. Its square base has four heavy arches in the form of a gate. Above each gate, you see a large crowned medallion with the chain of office of the Golden Fleece and in the middle, the Belgian Lion. On the corners are the four symbols of the evangelists: the bull (Luke), the

The drum of the 'Reuzegom' refrain (photo: JvI).

lion (Mark), the eagle (John) and the angel (Matthew), all winged and with an opened bible.

Above this begins the richly detailed eight-cornered peak itself, with eight angels depicted as caryatids. These heavenly messengers hold respectively a songbook, an Irish harp, a double flute, a tambourine, cymbals, a hand organ, a viol and a lute. The angels and the evangelists were made in the atelier of Leuven sculptor Jozef van Uytvanck.

Then you see a small corridor with parapet, and the cut-away lantern with stone cupola and weathervane. The 7-metre high weathervane is made of wrought iron and copper. The gilded Belgian lion measures 1.25 metres. The cut-away gilded ball has a diameter of 1 metre. It weighs a total of 1,500 kilograms and was made in the ateliers of *Sillen Sizaire* of Heverlee. In 2002, the weathervane was fully restored by ornamental metalworker Dirk van der Loeff. The carillon originally consisted of 48 bells, again corresponding to the number of states that were part of the United States at the time. It weighs a total of 31,751 kilograms. Edward Dean Adams (1846-1931), designer of the *Niagara Falls Power Company* and driving force behind the *Engineering Foundation*, took the initiative to present carillon and tower clock to the Leuven university as a tribute to the American engineers killed during the First World War. The carillon was designed by Frederick Christian Mayer (1882-1973), organist and choir director of the famous American military academy at West Point. The bells were cast by the English company mentioned above, *Gillett & Johnston*, a work that normally takes two years but was handled in an absolute record time of less than six months. The company received the assignment in December 1927, and on 18 May 1928 the carillon was played for the first time at the bell-foundry by Denijn, in the presence of the American and Belgian ambassadors and the mayors of London and Leuven.

The large bourdon, *The Liberty Bell of Louvain*, which rings on the hour, weighs 7,096 kilograms and bears the following text on its front:

> This Carillon in Memory of the Engineers of the United States of America Who gave their Lives in the Service of their Country and its Allies in The Great War 1914-1918.

The carillon needed a thorough renovation at the beginning of the 1980s. American university carilloneur Margo Halsted sounded the alarm bell(!) and on 7 October 1983, the renovated carillon was played for the first time. The costs of the renovation, executed by the *Royal Eijsbouts* bell-foundry from Asten (the Netherlands), were borne by American engineer associations, and countless Belgian and foreign private and official sponsors.

The carillon was then expanded with recast and new bells. It now has 63 bells and weighs 35,394 kilograms. For a number of years, the Leuven carillon was the largest in Europe, until Berlin outdid Leuven in 1987 with a carillon consisting of 68 bells. In addition, in 1998, 16 of the original small bells from the library carillon were used to make an automatic carillon for Saint John the Baptist Church in the Leuven Grand Beguinage.

The Liberty Bell of Louvain (photo: University Archives).

It is also interesting to know that the largest of the newly cast bells carries this universal message:

INTERPRES VARIAE SVM VITAE VOCE SONORA:
FORTVNAM CELEBRO SIT BONA SITVE MALA.
SIT PAX IN TERRIS, CONCORDIA REGNET IN ORBE:
EX ALTO CVNCTIS HAEC PIA VOTA CANO.

(translation: Interpreter of changing life am I, with harmonious voice;
I celebrate the fate of people in good and bad times.
Let there be peace on earth, let harmony govern the world:
From the tower I peal this pious wish for all.)[4]

University carilloneur Luc Rombouts regularly performs concerts. According to experts, the Leuven carillon is one of the best in the world.

GROUND FLOOR

The ground floor consists of a beautiful double gallery with eighteen round and two octagonal pillars supporting gothic ribbed vaults. Immediately in front of you, behind the double glass door, is the reception counter. The corridor is recessed here. Behind the counter, you see the double wooden door with wrought-iron gate of the exhibition hall. To the left of this door, a large commemorative plaque in green marble has been hung. It is the inauguration plaque of 4 July 1928:

This Library, which the American People in their Admiration for His Eminence Cardinal Mercier, His Majesty King Albert and the Belgian Nation, Presented to the University of Louvain, was inaugurated on July IV – MCMXXVIII under the Rectorate of

4. Translator's note: Author of the Latin text was Jozef IJsewijn (1932-1998), world-renowned professor of Latin at the KU Leuven

Mgr Paulin Ladeuze. Designed by Messrs Warren & Wetmore and built by the Foundation Company.

To the right of this door you see a second inscription, also chiselled in green marble. It is a memorial to the work of the *Commission for Relief in Belgium*, with Herbert Hoover as chair. During the First World War, this commission collected food and clothing in England and the United States for the destitute Belgian population. To the right is the door that opens onto the inner courtyard. When the weather is nice, you can rest here for a while. Leaving the inner courtyard, you see on the left, next to the counter, a model of the carillon tower, in painted wood and plaster. This model comes from the atelier of sculptor Jozef van Uytvanck.

To the left of the counter begins the monumental staircase that leads to the first floor. The style of the pillars and arches of the gallery as well as the large staircase refer strongly to the lower floor halls of the Universiteitshal on Naamsestraat where, until World War I, the University Library was also housed (see photo p. 54).

Immediately to the right of the first step of the Grand Staircase, at the top, you see the name of a quite special benefactor of the library: the *Police Department of the City of New York*. Evidently, there were many book friends among the New York police at the time. Before you go upstairs, perhaps it is best to peek at the Tower Courtyard, which can be reached via the first wooden door to the left of the Grand Staircase. Located here is the remnant of the second part of the infamous letter balustrade (*Furore Teutonico diruta, dono Americano restituta*), which was never installed on the facade (see p. 33).

The only remaining five letters of the infamous letter balustrade. They constitute the end of the second part of the inscription, ITUTA, i.e. the final letters of RESTITUTA (photo: JvI).

GRAND STAIRCASE AND FIRST FLOOR HALL

The Grand Staircase has pillars with lions' heads and is made of solid polished limestone, probably Savonnières. This honorary stairwell is located in the lower building of the carillon tower. On the wall on the right side of the first part, you see a large inscription, a memorial to the gift of the carillon and tower clock by the American engineers associations to the Leuven University. Above, half way up the double landing, is the bronze bust of Herbert Clark Hoover, the driving force behind the financing of the new University library. The bust is the work of Suzanne Farnam-Silvercruys (1898-1973), daughter of Belgian diplomat Baron François Silvercruys, who had

The walkway on the ground floor, before the glass wall and the cloakroom were installed in 1986 (photo: University Archives).

established herself as artist in the United States. Hoover received an honorary doctorate from Leuven in 1924.

You now arrive in the Hall between the former Catalogue Room and the Main Reading Room. This central hall, the heart of the building, measures 13 metres by 8.40 metres. Immediately to the right you see a bronze bell. It is a smaller copy of *The Liberty Bell of Louvain* in the bell tower. It is rung each evening to announce the closing of the library.

In front of it is a large plaster statue of an angel. This is a model for the basilica of Koekelberg, from the hand of Danish-Belgian artist Harry Elstrøm (1906-1993), also professor at the Leuven faculty of Applied Sciences. Other plaster models by him can be found elsewhere in the building. Elstrøm is also famous as a designer of coins and pennies, such as the old twenty-franc piece bearing the image of King Boudewijn.

Across from the angel, on the other side of the hall, is the bronze bust of Emile Francqui (1863-1935), made by well-known Belgian sculptor Jules Lagae (1862-1931). The free-thinking explorer, banker and politician Francqui played a major role in the construction of the new university library, among others as a member of the *Commission for Relief in Belgium Educational Foundation*. He founded the University Foundation and the National Fund for Scientific Research (NFWO in Dutch). He became an honorary doctor of this university in 1921.

Bust of Herbert Hoover (photo: JvI).

As inscription you read:

Émile Francqui/ Ministre d'état/ Créateur de la Fondation Universitaire/ Docteur honoris causa de l'Université/ 1863-1935.

(translation: Émile Francqui/ minister of state/ Founder of the University Foundation/ honorary doctor of the University/ 1863-1935.)

To the left and right of the large double door of the former Catalogue Room, and to the right of the double door to the Main Reading Room, hang three large paintings by the Brussels painter

Albert Ciamberlani (1864-1956). They are preliminary designs, tempera on cardboard and oil (distemper) on canvas, for three of the large mosaics located in the peristylium of the triumphal arch at the Brussels Cinquantenaire. The general title of this work is: *Tribute to the heroes who died for the fatherland during the war of 1914-1918.* The mosaics were completed in 1931. On the design at the right, on the Catalogue Room side, you see three figures that represent, from left to right: *the Hope of Immortality* , the Greek poet of war songs *Tyrtaeus* and *Immortality.* Allegorically portrayed on the design to the left are: *Taking Leave of the Past, the Echo of History, Historiography, the Crowning of Great Deeds* and *a Bucolic Singer.*

Bust of Emile Francqui (photo: JvI).

The third design on the Main Reading Room side again depicts an allegory, which is described as *Glorious Procession for the Crowning of the Illustrious Past.*

To the left of the double door to the Main Reading Room you see a bronze commemorative plaque that was added in 1964 containing the portrait of head librarian Etienne van Cauwenbergh. This commemorative plaque was designed by Harry Elstrøm. The Latin text reads as follows:

ILLVSTRISSIMO DOMINO DOMINO
STEPHANO VAN CAVWENBERGH
★MDCCCXC MCMLXIV+ PER ANNOS QVADRAGINTA
DVOS BIBLIOTHECAE VNIVERSITATIS CATHOLICAE
LOVANIENSIS PRAEFECTO BENE MERITO.
DIRVIT HANC BIS FLAMMA DOMVM MAVORTE FVRENTE
RESTITVIT STEPHANVS QVO FVIT ANTE DECVS

(translation: To the Very Reverend Monsignor Etienne van Cauwenbergh,[5] 1890 – 1964 +, meritorious director, for forty-two years, of the Library of the Catholic University of Louvain. This house was destroyed by fire twice amidst the violence of war; Etienne restored it to its former splendour.)

Above the double door to the Main Reading Room you see a copper representation of *Sedes Sapientiae*, from the hand of sculptor Jacques Moeschal. Below it you read a verse[6], left in Latin and right in Greek, from the Bible:

SAPIENTIA AEDIFICAVIT SIBI DOMVM
ΜΕΤΑ ΣΟΦΙΑΣ ΟΙΚΟΔΟΜΕΙΤΑΙ ΟΙΚΟΣ

(translation: Wisdom has built itself a house/ With wisdom a house is built)

These proverbs were displayed above the main entrance to the Universiteitshal in the seventeenth century.

5. Translator's note: author of the Latin text is Jozef IJsewijn (see above). The verses form an elegiac distich (= hexameter + pentameter). *Mavors* is the archaic, poetic name of the god of war Mars. *Stephanus* = Etienne.
6. Translator's note: Proverbs 9: 1, in the Vulgate translation. Across from the Latin text is the Greek Septuagint translation of Proverbs 24: 3 (!): 'With wisdom a house is built'.

Commemorative plaque of Etienne van Cauwenbergh (photo: JvI).

MAIN READING ROOM

You now enter the Main Reading Room, 44 metres long and 13 metres wide, with two smaller reading rooms left and right, each 12 metres deep and 13 metres wide. The original reading room from 1928 had barrel vaulting and only 1 gallery (see photo p. 34). It was decorated with the flags of the great American universities that had contributed to the financing of the new University Library. The room was completely destroyed in 1940 and thus had to be refurnished. The renovation was done in 1950-1951.

Architect Henry Lacoste, successor to world-famous Victor Horta (1861-1947) at the Brussels Academy, designed the plans for the new reading room. He replaced the barrel vaulting by a flat concrete ceiling that supports two new floors above it. He also added a second

The double entrance door to the Main Reading Room (photo: JvI).

gallery over the entire length and the two sides, so that the total length of the book racks was drastically increased to around 500 metres. Today there are general and specialised reference works available to the reader (19,774 different titles from the 18th, 19th, 20th and 21st centuries). The focus of these collections is principally the human sciences. Here you will find – as is the case elsewhere in the building – PCs with which the reader can consult the online catalogue, as well as digital reference works, e-books, databases, full text journals and the internet. The Wi-Fi zone of the Main Reading Room for that matter is one of the hottest hot spots of the entire KU Leuven. The interior is abundantly clad in high-quality robust oak, which provides the totality with a warm, rich and very academic feel. This cabinetwork was installed by the Brussels firm *Pernet*.

It is not easy to define exactly the style of the interior. We find traces of classical and African motifs as well as art deco. The oak tables and chairs, however, are faithful copies of the pre-war originals, designed by architect Warren. The conspicuous lighting fixtures with fluorescent lamps, 28 in total, were made and provided by the *Philips* branch in Leuven, which has disappeared in the meantime. The large clock at the top, right of the lending counter, is electrically driven by a modern Swiss system made by the firm *FAVAG* from Neuchâtel. Across from the clock, on the other short side of the room, you see a monumental figure of Christ on the cross.

Jacques Moeschal carved the handrails, as well as the two panels on the balustrade of the first gallery. One panel depicts a chemistry student in a laboratory, the other an architecture student at a drawing table. The other panels were never finished.

The start of the handrail, on the Arendstraat side, consists of an eagle with a monstrous snake in a fatal hold between its strong claws and beak. The artist signed his work here with: J. Moeschal

The Main Reading Room today. More than 100,000 readers find their way to this library every year. It is also one of the universities most successful wireless internet (WiFi) environments. (photo: Dirk Motmans).

sculpsit – 1950. The body of this monster extends across the entire length of the first gallery. At the start of the other handrail, you see a fearless lion restraining the tail of the monster. The eagle is American, the snake German and the lion Belgian. Some visitors will perhaps remember Moeschal's daring *Arrow of Civil Engineering* at the 1958 World Fair in Brussels.

On the windowsills are a number of busts. From left to right you recognise:

Raymond M. Lemaire (1921-1997), professor of architectural history, bronze from 1996.
Raymond Lemaire (1878-1954), professor of architectural history, plaster from 1945, by Oscar de Clerck (1892-1968).

Carved handrail: Eagle and snake (photo: JvI).

Carved handrail: Lion with the tail of a snake (photo: JvI).

Jean Baptiste Carnoy (1836-1899), professor of biology, plaster, by Jules Lagae (1862-1931).

André Dumont (1847-1920), professor of mining engineering and discoverer of the coal basin in the Kempen region of Belgium, plaster with bronze patina, by Thomas Vinçotte (1850-1925).

Pierre Craninx (1805-1890), professor of internal medicine, plaster, unknown sculptor.

Pierre François Xavier de Ram (1804-1865), professor of history and rector, plaster from 1866, by Herman de Fierlandt (1835-1872).

Cornelius R.A. van Bommel (1790-1852), bishop of Liège, co-founder of the Catholic University in 1834, plaster, unknown sculptor.

Albert Carnoy (1878-1961), professor of Greek language and literature, general linguistics etc., senator and minister, plaster with bronze patina from 1962, by Marcel Kok.

Louis Henry (1834-1913), professor of geology, mineralogy and chemistry, plaster with bronze patina from 1900, by Franz Vermeylen (1857-1922).

Antoine Joseph Haine (1825-1900), professor of theology, plaster from 1896, by Jean Hodru (1870-1932).

Nicholas Murray Butler (1862-1947), President of Columbia University, bronze from 1923, by Pierre de Soete (1886-1948).

In the smaller reading room (the Ladeuze Room) on the Blijde-Inkomststraat side, hangs the portrait of rector Paulin Ladeuze, oil

Balustrade first gallery: architecture student (photo: JvI).

Balustrade first gallery: chemistry student (photo: JvI).

on canvas, painted by Jozef Janssens (1854-1930). The text in the wooden wainscoting below reads as follows:

PAVLINVS LADEVZE EPISCOPVS TIBERIENSIS REC-
TOR MAGNIFICVS MCMIX MCMXL.
OPVS JOSEPHI JANSSENS A[NNO] MCMXXXVIII.

(translation: Paulin Ladeuze, bishop of Tiberias, rector magnifi-
cus, 1909-1940. A work by Joseph Janssens, in the year 1938.)

The upper right corner of the painting contains the coat of arms of Ladeuze as titular bishop of Tiberias, an honorary title with as imaginary diocese the biblical lake of the same name in the Holy Land. The canvas was signed and dated at the lower left: Jozef (sic) Janssens/ 1927. The inscription below it, dated 1938, is therefore wrong. Until the Second World War, this painting hung in the Hall between the Main Reading Room and the Catalogue Room, and survived the fire.

In the other smaller reading room (the Mercier Room) on the Arendstraat side, hangs the portrait of Joseph Désiré Cardinal Mercier (1851-1926), oil on canvas, a work by the French painter Albert Besnard (1849-1934). To the left of Mercier you see Christ on the cross, and to the right, Leuven on fire. The cardinal is holding a pen in his right hand and a number of sheets of paper in his left hand. The gilded text on the black marble plaque below it reads as follows:

D. I. CARD. MERCIER ARCHIEP. MECHLINIEN.
MCMVI . MCMXXVI.
OPVS ALBERTI BESNARD MCMXXIII

(translation: Désiré Joseph Cardinal Mercier, archbishop of Mechelen, 1906-1926. A work by Albert Besnard, 1923.)

The artist signed the work at the middle right: *Besnard/ Rome 2 June 1916*. Thus the date 1923 according to the inscription below it is

Portrait of Cardinal Mercier by Albert Besnard (photo: Paul Stuyven).

incorrect. Mercier posed for Besnard in the Villa Medici in Rome. In his left hand, he holds the text of his notorious pastoral letter of Christmas 1914, in which he riled the German occupying forces.

In it he declared: '*This power* (German – JvI)) *has no legal authority. And consequently, in the depths of your soul, you do not owe reverence, or loyalty, or obedience to it.*' The letter was read aloud in all churches. In fact, for his persistent resistance, Mercier was summoned to Rome in 1916 to be carpeted. The canvas hung in the Hall between the Main Reading Room and the Catalogue Room until the Second World War, and – like the portrait of Ladeuze – survived the fire.

On the windowsills are a number of busts in plaster. Along the windows, on the Mgr. Ladeuzeplein side, you see from left to right three Belgian monarchs: Albert I (1875-1934), Leopold II (1835-1909) and Leopold III (1901-1983). On the window, to the right of the portrait of Mercier, is a plaster portrait of canon Jean Baptiste Carnoy, identical to the one in the Main Reading Room.

Finally, on the ceiling, on a corner section you see a painting depicting two winged horses above an 'ancient' city. The original intent was to have all of the sections in the Main Reading Room painted. However, it was limited to a single attempt. The painter is unknown.

When leaving the Main Reading Room, you proceed directly to the right into the passage behind the double swinging doors. Hanging on the wall is a work by Antwerp artist Denmark (1950): *Dood archief XII*, a work from 1981. It is a gift (2009) of the artist to the KU Leuven as a tribute to Rector Marc Vervenne (1949). You can also admire a plaster model with patina by Elstrøm: *The prisoner*, from 1942.

The spiral staircase at the end of the passage heads to the floor on which the Tabularium (Latin for the archives in ancient Rome) is located; this floor houses the library and reading rooms of the department of Manuscripts and Precious Works. This library contains a unique collection of specialised reference works on manuscripts, watermarks, paper, printing, typography, book illustration, bookbinding, publishing, libraries, cartography, graphic art and photography. The Tabularium is not included in our guided tour. However, if as reader you wish to look up something, you are of course very welcome to do so.

GRAND STAIRCASE AND SECOND FLOOR HALL

You now proceed back to the Hall and take the large staircase to the second floor, which is also located in the lower building of the bell tower. Here you can see four copper plates hanging on the landing. These contain the names of the institutions, associations, companies and persons who financed the restoration of the carillon in 1983. The restored carillon was re-inaugurated on 7 October of that year. Also have a look at the proud Belgian lion on the dividing point between the two handrails. It would also be difficult to miss the large – gilded and polychromed – wooden statue of Buddha. It was made in Myanmar around 1800, and belongs to the so-called Mandalay style. It was donated to the KU Leuven.

Ascending the second part of the staircase, you see in the upper right corner a beautiful cut-away bay with spiral staircase. The bay evokes images of the renaissance castles along the Loire. The spiral staircase leads to the top floors of the tower. The tower and carillon is open only to group visits and by appointment.

Grand staircase and bay (photo: JvI).

Entering the Hall on the second floor, you see on your left a painting, oil on canvas, and a plaster bust. The painting depicts a calvary. It is anonymous and is dated around 1600.

The bust portrays Robert de Kerchove (1846-1942), the first abbot of Keizersberg Abbey in Leuven, a work by Elstrøm from 1938. Directly to the right you notice a plaster model for a statue of Saint Bernard, also a work by Elstrøm, from 1943.

Behind it, to the right of the door to the carillon tower, you see an exceptionally large – 4.5 metres high – standing clock. The works and the clock face are probably from the hand of 18th century clockmaker C. G. de Behaigne, town watchmaker in Leuven. The cabinet is a somewhat hybrid design from after the Second World War, in which older elements were incorporated. The clock still runs and needs winding only once every two weeks.

In the meantime, you of course have already seen the four large plaster statues. They are sculptor's models of the four evangelists: John, Luke, Matthew and Mark. Elstrøm designed them between 1955 and 1963 for the portal of the basilica of Koekelberg.

Behind the impressive baroque door embellished with angels, you will find the East Asian library. The University established this library in 1996, and was the only library in Belgium to develop a special collection on China, Japan and Korea. In addition to the many works in the languages of this region, books in Western languages were also purchased to meet growing demand from a broad public. The library houses reference works and handbooks, as well as specific series, monographs, journals and databases needed in the context of scientific research. All visitors have access to fascinating material on language, culture, religion and society in the Far East.

Now take the wide, half-round staircase to the right across from the entrance to this library. On the right side of the staircase is a plaster model of one of the statues in the facade of the Leuven town hall. It depicts Matthias van den Gheyn (1721-1785), city carilloneur of Leuven and perhaps the most important composer ever of carillon music.

Here you will also find four oil paintings on canvas by the French painter François Flameng (1856-1923). These are the design sketches representing four giant paintings that until 1940 hung in the present-day Jubileumzaal of the restored University Hall. They depict German soldiers setting fire to the university library, the groundbreaking ceremony for the new university library, the Parnassus of Leuven professors and artists, and Portuguese humanist

Libellus vere aureus nec
MINVS SALVTARIS   QVAM FESTI-
uus de optimo reip. ftatu, deq̃ noua Infula Vtopia
authore clariffimo viro Thoma Moro inclytæ
ciuitatis Londinenfis ciue & vicecomite cu-
ra M. Petri Aegidii Antuerpiēfis, & arte
Theodorici Martini Aluftenfis, Ty
pographi almæ Louanienfium
Academiæ nunc primum
accuratiffime edi
tus,⁖

Title page of the first edition of Thomas More's Utopia, printed in 1516 by Dirk Martens in Leuven (photo: University Library).

1974, the Leuven student newspaper Veto *was established (photo: University Archives).*

Damião de Góis (1502-1574) defending the City of Leuven against Maarten van Rossum (1542) together with the students.

This floor also houses two small museums.

On display in the *Valerius Andreas Room* are manuscripts and old prints. You receive not only an overview of the history of the book and printing, but also of the rich history of this university. You will encounter great names from the Low Countries: Andreas Vesalius (1514-1564), the father of modern anatomy, Gerard Mercator (1512-1594), founder of modern cartography, and Leuven professor Justus Lipsius (1547-1606), classicist, philologist and historian. You can also admire letters by the humanists Desiderius Erasmus (1466-1536) and Thomas More (1478-1535), whose world-famous book Utopia was printed for the first time in 1516 in Leuven. The German church reformer Martin Luther (1483-1546) has a place as well; theologians from Leuven and Cologne after all were the first to publicly reject part of his theses in 1519. The Leuven index of prohibited books (1546) also deserves your attention. And don't forget Georges Lemaître (1894-1966), Leuven professor of physics and father of the big bang theory. This museum is open only to group visits and by appointment.

The _Museum For Flemish Student Life_ provides you with an overview of 100 years of student life in Leuven, from around 1870 to the beginning of the 1970s. This museum is also only open to group visits and by appointment.

CONCISE
BIBLIOGRAPHY

Albert Füglister, *Louvain: ville martyre,* Parijs, 1916.

Hugh S. Gibson, *A journal from our legation in Belgium,* New York, 1917.

Ed. de Moreau, *La bibliothèque de l'université de Louvain, 1636-1914,* Leuven, 1918.

Prosper Poullet, *La bibliothèque de Louvain. Séance commémorative du 4e anniversaire de l'incendie,* Parijs, 1919.

Brand Whitlock, *Belgium under the occupation: a personal narrative,* Londen 1919.

Oeuvre internationale de Louvain: bulletin publié par le Commissariat général, Leuven, 1919-1928.

Oeuvre internationale de Louvain. Commissariat général, La nouvelle bibliothèque de l'université, Leuven, 1929.

University library of Louvain. List of inscriptions on the walls and pilasters, Brugge, s.d.

Leo Van der Essen e.a., *Les crimes de guerre commis lors de l'invasion du territoire national. Mai 1940. La destruction de la bibliothèque de l'université de Louvain,* Luik, 1946.

[Jean Schoonjans], *Universiteitsbibliotheek. Een bijdrage tot haar geschiedenis,* Leuven, 1977.

[Brochure gedrukt n.a.v. de inzegening van de gerestaureerde Universiteitsbeiaard, 7 oktober 1983], Leuven, 1983.

Jan Roegiers, *Vijf eeuwen bibliotheekgeschiedenis,* in: *Ex officina,* 1 (1984), p. 7-13.

Jan F. Vanderheyden, *Het herstel van de Leuvense Universiteitsbibliotheek 1940-1945,* in: *Onze Alma Mater,* 41 (1987), 2, p. 119-139.

Mark Derez, *Leuven brandt: 25-26 augustus 1914,* brochure bij de tentoonstelling in de Centrale Bibliotheek, Leuven, 1989.

Wolfgang Schivelbusch, *Eine Ruine im Krieg der Geister. Die Bibliothek von Löwen August 1914 bis Mai 1940,* Frankfurt am Main, tweede herziene druk, 1993.

Chris Coppens e.a., *Leuven in books, Books in Leuven: the oldest university of the Low Countries and its library,* Leuven, 1999.

Het imaginaire museum van de Universiteitsbibliotheek, themanummer van *Ex officina:* nieuwsbrief van de Vrienden van de Universiteitsbibliotheek, 13 (2000), 1.

John Horne e.a., *German atrocities, 1914: a history of denial,* New Haven, 2001.

Chris Coppens, Marc Derez, Jan Roegiers, *Leuven University Library: 1425-2000,* Leuven, 2005.

Jo Tollebeek, Geert Vanpaemel, Mark Derez, *Album of a scientific world. The University of Louvain around 1900,* Leuven, 2012.

APPENDIX
LIST OF THE COMMEMORATIVE PLAQUES, STONES AND INSCRIPTIONS ON THE WALLS AND THE PILASTERS OF THE UNIVERSITY LIBRARY

The numbers after each inscription refer to the circled numbers on the map/diagram at the end, borrowed from the brochure *University library of Louvain. List of inscriptions on the walls and pilasters*, anonymously published shortly before the Second World War. These numbers should help in finding the more than 300 separate inscriptions. All inscriptions were checked on site, possibly translated and provided with a single designation. The 'Commemorative stones of Benefactors' (p. 116) are arranged according to the States of the U.S.A., in alphabetical order. Under each State are also the names of the benefactors in alphabetical order. The same applies to the 'Miscellaneous' at the very end (p. 129). The assistance of Andries Welkenhuysen was indispensable in all of this.

CHRONOGRAMS[7]

SANGVINIS AMERICI BELGII LIBERATIONIS
CAVSA PROFVSI RECORDATIONI PERENNI   8

1928: As a lasting memorial to the American blood that was shed for the liberation of Belgium.

SIDERVM CONCVRSV PHOENIX RECRESCIT   9

1928: When the stars hasten to help, the Phoenix rises again.
N.B. the stars: refer to the stars on the flag of the U.S.A.

IVRIS SERVATORIBVS ALBERTO MERCIER
BELGICAE NATIONI STATVS CONFOEDERATI   10

---

7. The author of these seven chronograms is Pierre Scheuer S.J. (1872-1957), lecturer and *scriptor* at the Leuven house of study of his order. See also footnote p. 22.

1928: To the defenders of justice Albert and Mercier, to the Belgian people: the United States.

+ LAPIS PRIMARIVS BIBLIOTHECAE LOVANIENSIS NOBILITER REFICIENDAE 19

1921: Foundation stone for the rebuilding in splendour of the Leuven Library.

IN FVNEREA NOCTE AMICA COLLVX-ERVNT SIDERA 79-85

1928: During the fatal night shone friendly the stars.
N.B. the stars: see above.

FACE CONSVMPTA FAX VNIVERSO ACCENDARIS IPSA 92-97

1928: May you who were consumed by the torch of war, yourself be a torch for all the world.

SVCCENDERVNT GENTIBVS LVMINAR IN SAECVLA 115

1928: For the peoples they lit a beacon for the centuries.

MEMORIALS

Commemorative plaque for the inauguration of 4 July 1928   69

This Library, which the American People in their Admiration for His Eminence Cardinal Mercier, His Majesty King Albert and the Belgian Nation, Presented to the University of Louvain, was inaugurated on July IV – MCMXXVIII under the Rectorate of Mgr Paulin Ladeuze. Designed by Messrs Warren & Wetmore and built by the Foundation Company.

Commemorative plaque in honour of the Commission for
Relief in Belgium Educational Foundation   72

To commemorate the work of the Commission for Relief in Belgium, Herbert Hoover, Chairman, for its share in safeguarding the health, assuring the food supply & maintaining the solidarity of the civilian population of Belgium during the Great War 1914-1918, And to acknowledge the Endowment given by the Commission for the support of this University in 1919 & gifts from the C.R.B. Educational Foundation, Inc. for the completion of this building from 1923 to 1928, This tablet was placed by the Catholic University of Louvain July 4 – 1928.

American Engineers' Memorial   154

In Memory of the Engineers of the Unites States of America Who gave their lives in the service of their Country & its Allies in the Great War 1914-1918, The Carillon & the Clock in this Tower have been given to the University of Louvain by members & friends of the American Society of Civil Engineers, American Institute of Mining & Metallurgical Engineers, The American Society of Mechanical Engineers, American Institute of Electrical Engineers, The Society of American Military Engineers, Army Ordnance Association, American Society of Naval Engineers, American Institute of Consulting Engineers, American Institute of Chemical Engineers, American Railway Engineering Association, American Society of Heating and Ventilating Engineers,

American Society of Refrigerating Engineers, Illuminating Engineering Society, Institute of Radio Engineers, Society of Automotive Engineers, Society of Naval Architects & Marine Engineers.

Carillon Givers' Memorial[8]

American Engineers Memorial Carillon & Clock made possible by the services and generosity of Edward Dean Adams and of those others whose names are inscribed in the stones of this tower: Edward G. Acheson, Kempton Adams, Pierpont Adams, W.H. Aldridge, A.W. Berresford, George S. Davison, Arthur S. Dwight, George W. Fuller, George Gibbs, William L. Honnold, L.R. Lohr, John Markle, James H. Mc Graw, Mc Graw Hill Publishing Co, Ambrose Swasey, Charles M. Schwab, Samuel M. Vauclain, Henry Walters, Roy V. Wright.

The Liberty Bell of Louvain[9]

The Liberty Bell of Louvain.
This Carillon in Memory of the Engineers of the United States of America Who gave their Lives in the Service of their Country and its Allies in The Great War 1914-1918. Presented by Members And friends of American Society of Civil Engineers, American Institute of Mining and Metallurgical Engineers, American Society of Mechanical Engineers, American Institute of Electrical Engineers and Associated Societies, July 4th, 1928.

Memorial Cardinal Mercier   20

CARDINALIS MERCIER STVDII GEN[ERALIS] LOVAN[IENSIS] MAG[ISTRI] PRIMATIS BELGII POPVLI SVI DVCTORIS AC PATRIAE AVSPICIS MEMORIAE DICATVM.

8. This inscription is located on the stone spiral staircase to the bell tower, on the side and the bottom of 19 steps. Thus it is only visible to visitors of the bell tower (only on request).
9. Bourdon in the tower, text on front and rear.

(translation: Dedicated to the memory of Cardinal Mercier, lecturer at the Leuven University, Primate of Belgium, leader of his people and visionary of the fatherland.)
N.B. Author of the Latin text is Pierre Scheuer (see above).

RESTORATION CARILLON 1983

Inscription new bourdon in the tower:[10]

UPPER RING

ANDREAS LEHR ASTENII ME FECIT IN OFFICINA AERARIA EYSBOUTS.

(translation: André Lehr has cast me in Asten at the Eijsbouts bronze foundry.)

SIDE, FRONT

BALDVINVS I BELGARVM REX ET FABIOLA REGINA
GODEFRIDVS CARDINALIS DANNEELS
CAROLVS H. PRICE II CIVITATVM AMERICAE
FOED[ERATARVM] ORATOR APVD BELGAS
PETRVS DE SOMER VNIVERSITATIS CATHOLICAE

LOVANIENSIS RECTOR
CAROLVS TAVERNIER VNIVERSITATIS GERENDAE
PRAEFECTVS

MARGARITA HALSTED COLLEGII CAMPANICINARII
LOVANIENSIS PRAESES

IOSEPHVS ROOSEMONT ARCHITECTVS
AEMILIVS L. BOVLPAEP OPERIS FVNDATI BELGOA
MERICANI EDVCATIONI FOVENDAE PRAESES
CAMPANAS RENOVATAS ITERVM DEDICAVERVNT
DIE VII MENSIS OCTOBRIS A[NNO] D[OMINI]
MCMLXXXIII.

10. Author of the Latin text is Jozef IJsewijn (see above). The four closing verses form two elegiac distichs; they continue in one full line above the striking ring.

(translation: Baudouin I, King of the Belgians, and Queen Fabiola, Godfried Cardinal Danneels, Charles H. Price II, ambassador of the United States of America in Belgium, Pieter De Somer, rector of the Katholieke Universiteit Leuven, Karel Tavernier, administrator-general of the University, Margo Halsted, chair of the Leuven Carillon Committee, architect Jos Roosemont, Emile L. Boulpaep, chair of the Belgian American Educational Foundation, have re-inaugurated the restored carillon on 7 October of the year of our Lord 1983.)

SIDE, REAR

HONORI ET MEMORIAE OMNIVM MACHINATORVM
E CIVITATIBVS AMERICAE FOEDERATIS
ORIVNDORVM
QVI
MARTE FVRENTE
SANGVINEM PRO PATRIA PROFVDERVNT.

(translation: To the honour and in memory of all engineers from the United States of America who shed their blood for the fatherland amidst the violence of war.)

LOWER RING

INTERPRES VARIAE SVM VITAE VOCE SONORA
FORTVNAM CELEBRO SIT BONA SITVE MALA.
SIT PAX IN TERRIS, CONCORDIA REGNET IN ORBE:
EX ALTO CVNCTIS HAEC PIA VOTA CANO.

(translation: Interpreter of changing life am I, with harmonious voice; I celebrate the fate of people in good and bad times. Let there be peace on earth, let harmony govern the world: from the tower I peal this pious wish for all.)

COMMEMORATIVE STONES OF BENEFACTORS

CALIFORNIA

COLORADO

CONNECTICUT

> This inscription is missing. The bronze medallion with
> inscription was taken from the wall (probably by thieves);
> only the chiselled decorative edging remains.

Yale University, New Haven   48
LVX ET VERITAS
(translation: Light and truth).
Motto on the coat of arms of Yale University.

ILLINOIS

INDIANA

KANSAS

MAINE

MARYLAND

MASSACHUSETTS

> TERRAS IRRADIENT
> (translation: Let them shine over the lands).
> Motto on the coat of arms of Amherst College.

MICHIGAN

MINNESOTA

MISSISSIPPI

MISSOURI

NEBRASKA

NEW HAMPSHIRE

NEW JERSEY

NEW YORK

IN LVMINE TVO VIDEBIMVS LVMEN
(translation: In Thy light shall we see the light)
= Psalm 39:10, motto of Columbia University.

OHIO

RHODE ISLAND

TENNESSEE

TEXAS

VERMONT

VIRGINIA

WASHINGTON

WASHINGTON, D.C.

WISCONSIN

MISCELLANEOUS